The Word in

Publications of the Joint Liturgical Group
established in 1963

The Renewal of Worship
The Calendar and Lectionary (1967)
The DailyOffice (1968)
    10th corrected impression (1973)
An Additional Lectionary (1969)
Holy Week Services (1971)
Initiation and Eucharist (1972)
Worship and the Child (1975)
The Daily Office Revised (1978)
Getting the Liturgy Right (1982)
Holy Week Services: Revised and expanded edition (1983)

The Word in Season

✠

*Essays by members of the
Joint Liturgical Group on the
use of the bible in liturgy*

edited by
Donald Gray

The Canterbury Press Norwich

The Canterbury Press Norwich, St Mary's Works,
St Mary's Plain, Norwich, Norfolk NR3 3BH

The Canterbury Press Norwich is a publishing imprint
of Hymns Ancient & Modern Limited

Cover design by Richard Morgan

ISBN 1 85311 001 9

First published 1988

© The Joint Liturgical Group

Filmset by Eta Services (Typesetters) Ltd, Beccles, Suffolk
Printed and Bound in Great Britain by
William Clowes Ltd, Beccles and London

Contents

Members of the Joint Liturgical Group 1988

The Church of England
The Rev. Canon Dr D. C. Gray (Secretary)
The Rev. M. R. Vasey

The Church of Scotland
The Rev. C. Robertson
The Rev. A. Scobie

The Baptist Union of Great Britain and Ireland
The Rev. N. Clark
The Rev. M. F. Williams

The United Reformed Church
The Rev. Dr C. P. Thompson
The Rev. J. Wyatt

The Episcopal Church in Scotland
The Rev. Dr G. Tellini

The Methodist Church
The Rev. A. R. George (Chairman)
The Rev. Dr G. S. Wakefield

The Roman Catholic Church
The Rev. P. M. Gallacher
The Rev. E. Matthews

The Fellowship of the Churches of Christ
The Rev. E. G. Greer

During the compilation of this book the Rev. David Beckett and the Rev. J. C. Stewart were representatives of the Church of Scotland, Canon H. E. Winstone of the Roman Catholic Church, the Rev. V. L. Hunter of the Fellowship of the Churches of Christ, the Rev. Donald McIllhagga of the United Reformed Church, and Canon Professor D. R. Jones of the Church of England.

1

INTRODUCTION TO A DEBATE

✠

Donald Gray

Among the first tasks that the interdenominational Joint
Liturgical Group set itself was the planning of a calendar
and a lectionary, and the results of its deliberations on that
subject were published as *The Calendar and Lectionary* in
1967.[1]

Those recommendations have been widely influential in
the work of liturgical revision among the churches in Great
Britain and in other English-speaking countries. The
Church of England, with just a few modifications, used it in
its *Alternative Service Book 1980*, the Methodist Church in
The Methodist Service Book, 1975, the United Reformed
Church in *A Book of Services*, 1980, and the Church of
Scotland in *The Book of Common Order*, 1979. A number of
provinces of the Anglican Communion have included it in
their official publications for worship.

Of the churches represented in the Joint Liturgical Group
the Roman Catholic Church was notable in not using the
material at all. They already had a revised Calendar and
Lectionary based on principles contained in *Constitution on
the Sacred Liturgy* which was part of the Vatican II liturgical reforms. Whereas the JLG's recommendations were
novel in proposing a two-year cycle of lections, the new
Roman Lectionary had decided to spread material over
three years.

This Lectionary proved to have attractions outside the
Roman Communion, not least in the USA, and addition-
ally the Lambeth Conference of 1978 made a strong recommendation to the provinces of the Anglican Communion

that they should consider this alternative.[2] The Anglican Church in the United States (ECUSA) officially adopted the Roman Lectionary as an authorised alternative, but also took part in an ecumenical exploration to see if agreement could be reached across the denominations on a shared lectionary.

This was achieved through the work of the Consultation on Common Texts (CCT) and published as *Common Lectionary* in 1983.[3]

In 1983 an ecumenical consultation, sponsored by CCT and ICEL,[4] was held in Vienna before the congress of *Societas Liturgica*. The consultation resolved to support the formation of an international English-speaking consultative group on an ecumenical basis which would discuss liturgical matters of common interest. Such a body was duly formed under the title The English Language Liturgical Consultation (ELLC). Among the tasks that this Consultation set itself as a result of its first full meeting in Boston, Mass. in 1985 was a review of the liturgical texts prepared by the International Consultation on English Texts (ICET)[5] (this body had not met since 1974) and to seek to assist in bringing about an international ecumenical lectionary.[6]

This latest piece of work by the British Joint Liturgical Group is intended to be a contribution to this work. JLG from the outset has taken a full part in the work of ELLC, a decision having been made that representation on this new consultation should be from ecumenical liturgical bodies rather than from individual churches.[7]

In our book we have attempted to go back to first principles and to discuss the *rationale* both for an ordered Calendar and a structured Lectionary. Our thoughts on these matters come just twenty years after the publication of the Group's earlier recommendation in *The Calendar and Lectionary*. We trust that we will not be accused of "liturgical fidgeting"; we are simply anxious that the material for the current debate should be as widely available as possible.

NOTES

1 This was supplemented by *An Additional Lectionary for use at a Second Sunday Service* in 1969. See A. R. George, p. 111 ff. *infra*.

2 *Report of the Lambeth Conference 1978*, no. 24, p. 47. In 1984 The General
   Synod of the Church of England, after receiving a report from its Liturgical
   Commission, *A Common Lectionary*, GS603, 1983, decided not to authorise the
   Roman Lectionary for Sundays as a permitted alternative. ASB contains the
   RC daily eucharistic lectionary, Table 4, p. 1071 ff.

3 *Common Lectionary. The Lectionary Proposed by the Consultation on Common
   Texts*, The Church Hymnal Corporation, 800 Second Avenue, New York,
   NY 10017, 1983.

4 The International Commission on English in the Liturgy is a joint Commission
   of the Catholic Bishops' Conference. Formed in 1963, since 1981 it has been engaged in a comprehensive programme of revising the liturgical texts which were
   the first fruits of *The Constitution on the Divine Liturgy*.

5 *Prayers We Have in Common*, Agreed Liturgical texts prepared by the International Consultation on English Texts. 2nd revised ed., Philadelphia, 1975.

6 The work of the formation of ELLC is described by one of its co-chairpersons
   Horace T. Allan in *Worship*, vol. 60, no. 2, pp. 172 ff.

7 I.e. Australian Consultation on the Liturgy (ACOL), the North American Con-
   sultation on Common Texts (CCT), the Liturgical Committee of the South
   African Church Unity Commission, the Joint Liturgical Consultation in New
   Zealand (JLC-NZ) and the British JLG.

2

WHY THE BIBLE?

✠

Colin P. Thompson

"Why must we always have the Bible read in services?"
That this question is asked at all is symptomatic of a
gradual change which has been taking place in our culture
over many years. The Bible has lost its centrality. Its stories,
characters, and teachings are no longer part of our general
knowledge, and it lies neglected on our shelves.

There are many reasons for this. The rise of the natural
sciences has provided an alternative account of the world in
which we live, from which divine intervention and miracle,
so much taken for granted in the Bible, have been excluded.
We can no longer picture heaven and hell as the Bible does,
nor do we think of illness as the work of demons and evil
spirits. Critical scholarship of the Biblical text has questioned the historical reliability of important parts of it, and
shown it to be at the mercy of human factors. These factors
have particularly affected the Creation and Fall stories of
Genesis and the cycles of stories about the Patriarchs
(Abraham, Isaac, Jacob, Joseph, Moses); and the Gospels
themselves have not emerged unscathed. All this has led
people to see the Bible as relative, arising out of particular
cultural contexts, and made it hard for them to accept it as
authoritative, divinely inspired or infallible.

At the same time as the traditional view of the Bible has
been undermined, familiarity with it has decreased. To
many people it speaks an almost incomprehensible
language: it comes to them as a stranger with the voice of
the ancient Near East, a literary and religious relic stranded
in the twentieth century yet expected to be of relevance to

life now. It has an alien, primitive feel, and is an embarrassment rather than an aid, especially where it contains material which is cruel, violent and blood-thirsty. The fact that it is now widely available in modern translations only highlights the problem: ancient literature conserves a majesty through the noble cadences of the past, whereas in our own idiom the gulf between the Bible's world and ours is even more sharply exposed.

Reactions to this vary among Christians. Some see no difficulty at all. They accept the Bible as the infallible word of God, believe it to be preserved from all error, and receive it as a divinely-given guide through all the perplexities of life. Where science appears to contradict it, science is in error; where scholars stress its human origins and confusions, it is they who are confused. Others, while recognising that the Bible contains many profound insights, do not understand why it alone must be the book of the Church's worship. They point to the great treasures of non-Biblical literature and find that these have power to illuminate their spiritual quest more powerfully and directly. They wonder why they may not have an equal claim on the Church's attention, especially since critical scholarship has questioned the uniqueness of the Bible and since it appears itself to contain an arbitrary selection of texts. Between such reactions lies a whole range of attitudes, and expressions like "the authority" or "the inspiration of Scripture" are made to carry widely varying meanings.

Though much excellent work has been done to restate the significance of the Bible for the Church today, it has not always filtered through to individual Christians. And although the sense of strangeness many people feel when they approach the Bible would be much lessened if they read it regularly, it is appropriate to explain why the Bible remains primary to Christian faith and worship, and why no other literature, however sublime, can take its place, though it may provide great inspiration.

The thirty-nine books of the Old Testament and the twenty-seven of the New form the canon of Christian Scripture. The word "canon" has nothing to do with weapons or ecclesiastical dignitaries: it comes from a Greek word meaning "measuring rod" and hence "standard" or "norm". The Old Testament, common to Jews and Christians, contains books of law, story, history, prophecy and wisdom, in poetry and prose, spanning a thousand years of the history of the Ancient Near East and recording even older traditions. The New Testament, with its four Gospels, the Acts of the Apostles, twenty-one letters and the Book of Revelation, belongs as a series of written documents to a much shorter period, a century or less. It centres entirely on the person and work of Jesus Christ and the life of the first Christian communities scattered across the Roman Empire. But both collections took a long time to reach their final, fixed state. The gradual formation of a new corpus of writings alongside the sacred literature of the Jewish people reflects the emergence of Christianity from a faith born within Judaism to one acquiring a quite separate identity.

For Christ and his apostles, and for the New Testament writers, "the Scriptures" meant the Old Testament. Jesus himself knew the whole of it: the phrase "from Abel to Zechariah" in Matt. 23.35/Luke 11.51 means "from Genesis to Chronicles", the first and last books of the Old Testament in the Hebrew order. The New Testament writers assumed a deep knowledge of the Old, and not only do they quote from it, they frequently allude to its language and theology without our realizing this.

The Old Testament canon was probably not fixed until the end of the first century A.D., and even then there were variations which continued to be a source of disagreement in later Christian history. The Greek-speaking Jews of the Diaspora regarded a number of books in Greek as inspired – prophecies, tales and wisdom books dating roughly from the period between the two Testaments. Some Fathers, like Augustine, accepted these as canonical; others, like Jerome, accepted only the Hebrew books, and called the Greek ones "ecclesiastical books". In the sixteenth century they were generally rejected by the Reformers, but the Council of Trent affirmed them as canonical in the Roman Catholic Church. Some of those Churches which rejected them as canonical Scripture (from which alone doctrine can be established) nevertheless accorded them spiritual value as books helping us in the way we are to live. Article VI of the Thirty-Nine Articles of the Church of England takes this view, following Jerome. That is why Roman Catholic versions include the Apocrypha (as it is called in common usage), whereas many other versions will sometimes omit it.

Already in the New Testament there are signs that Christian writings were acquiring a special place alongside "the Scriptures" (2 Peter 3.15–16). But not for some three hundred years after the death of Christ was the precise content of the New Testament settled. Some writings accepted in some places were excluded from the canon; others, such as Hebrews and Revelation, were included, though their position had been questioned from time to time. In this respect the history of the New Testament canon parallels the Old, since there had been differences of opinion on the inclusion of books such as Ecclesiastes and the Song of Solomon.

Since it is a great mistake to think of the canon as fixed and universally acknowledged from the beginning, the history of its formation raises problems almost as acute as those of the Biblical text itself. What processes led to some books being admitted and others not? Where were the lines drawn, and for what reasons? Many of the New Testament books seem to have been accepted on their own authority, both in terms of content and recognised authorship. Some were included because they came to be ascribed to an author whose credentials were beyond dispute, such as one of the apostles. For a long time now critical scholarship has questioned such attributions and undermined their authority, and we have to face the fact that we would proceed on a very different basis. Other books were accepted because they were judged orthodox, consistent with the faith taught by the apostles, or because they were widely used and revered in the worship of Christian congregations all over the Empire.

This makes it quite clear that the canon was the result of the Church's judgement, reached according to its best understanding, and, so it believed, under the guidance of the Holy Spirit.

The Church precedes the Bible, both for the obvious

reason that there was a Church before any of the New Testament books were written, and for the less obvious one that the Church established the canon and gave us the fixed body of sacred literature we call Holy Scripture. We may or may not be comfortable with the processes which brought this about, but the conclusion is inescapable: the Bible is first the result of faith, and only then its transmitter and producer. It is the first record, the foundation document, of the faith which Christians held, and contains the judgement of the community of faith, in obedience to the Holy Spirit, concerning those books which were the closest witnesses to that faith, not an arbitrary decision between works of equal merit. It is for such reasons that we call the Bible *normative*, a measure for the life of the Church, a constant correction and inspiration for every member of the community of faith.

What do we mean when we say that the Bible is the first *witness* to the Christian faith? The New Testament brings us into immediate contact with those who knew and followed Jesus of Nazareth, and with the impression he left on the first generation of Christians. Many parts of it preserve sayings and teachings of Jesus, or stories about him which derive directly from him or from his first apostles. There can be no substitute for this, as our age, so alert to the significance of historical origins and roots, may readily appreciate. In the first years of the Christian community there were eye-witnesses who could remember what Jesus had said and done, and as some of them at least believed that the world would end quite soon, there was little incentive to write down these accounts. But as the generation of eye-witnesses died out, it became imperative to write down "the things concerning Jesus" as they had been remembered and told. In the Gospels therefore we meet Jesus as his first followers recalled him, and as they considered the meaning of his death and resurrection for individuals and for the Church, a process which the Epistles (some of which are earlier in date than the Gospels) explore in great depth. The Epistles also give us a vivid and realistic picture of the struggles of the earliest Christian communities. The importance of the eye-witness account is stressed in the New

Testament itself (John 19.35, 21.24; 1 Cor. 15.6). Paul regards himself as the first among those who have met the risen and ascended Lord without having known him in his life on earth (1 Cor. 15.8), yet he himself stresses the succession of apostolic teaching and experience.

In this respect the New Testament contrasts strikingly with literature based loosely on a historical event or person, seen through the mists of intervening centuries and almost divorced from its historical roots – the Arthurian legends, *The Song of Roland*. Such works may have great imaginative and emotional power and appeal, but the New Testament is not like them. It is historically close to the events it described, in many cases within living memory, and cannot be dismissed as fabrication. Christianity is rooted as to its origins in a particular place, time, culture, person. What some have seen as the "scandal of particularity" (why should God choose to become incarnate in a particular time and place?) is a cause of rejoicing for humans, since we are all caught in one particularity or another, and always subject to its limitations, those of first-century Palestine or late twentieth-century Britain. The Bible witnesses to a God who is discerned through people and events rather than abstractions and theories. It is full of names: Abraham, Joseph, Moses, David, Jesus, Paul; Ur, Egypt, Canaan, Jerusalem, Galilee, Calvary, Damascus, Rome. The Incarnation is the fulness of the process whereby the eternal gives himself to be known in time and history, by himself assuming human existence.

This is not to say that the Bible as a whole, or even the New Testament, is historically accurate in every detail, in the way we imagine we are able to be when recording particular events. It comes to us from an ancient culture which did not approach history like that, but which thought that stories and symbolic language were as capable of communicating the truth – if not more so – than the language of facts and figures. Even our own time, with all its insistence on "getting at the facts", finds it hard to establish what they are, and even more so what they might mean, especially when they concern our "enemies". What is the truth about current events in Central America, for example? What was the truth about the sinking of the *General Belgrano* during the Falklands conflict? How do we know which voice to believe? You only have to read accounts of the same event from different points of view to see how interpretation, ideology and propaganda, subtle or crude, interpose between the event and us, and colour even the selection and presentation of the "facts". "Why is it", a Russian girl studying in this country once asked me, "that you hear only the bad news from the Soviet Union?" It was hardly sufficient to reply that we hear only bad news, full stop.

The "facts" of the Bible are not really in dispute: the emergence of a people with a distinctive identity, faith and sense of mission out of the shadowy world of the ancient Near East; their eventual settling in Canaan, their struggles, triumphs and disasters, their continuity through persecution, foreign domination and exile; the birth of a man of that people called Jesus in the reign of Tiberius Caesar; his ministry of teaching and healing; his subsequent crucifixion under Pontius Pilate; the emergence of a community within Judaism which believed him to be the promised Messiah, and risen from the dead. These things and many others in both Testaments are well enough attested by external evidence, when this is available, as in contemporary historians and in archaeology. But not everything which reads like "facts" in the Bible is to be understood in the same way: the first chapters of Genesis are a case in point. We have lost a sensitivity to language, and its many modes and levels of communication, which hinders our readings of the Bible.

For it is rarely history for its own sake. It carries interpretation, bears a message, asks for a response, and sees history as within the encompassing span of the purposes of God. Christian faith is not confined to the historical facts about Jesus: the Nicene Creed, for example, following the Biblical witness, proclaims that *for us men and for our salvation he came down from heaven*; that *by the power of the Holy Spirit he became man*; that *for our sake* he was crucified under Pontius Pilate. When we move to resurrection and ascension, the gift of the Holy Spirit, and the sacramental life of the Church, we find ourselves called to faith, and not to be explorers of the past, The Bible, then, is a witness to the meaning of the facts about Jesus of Nazareth, for it points beyond them and into their heart to discover there the Christ of God.

Deprived of this witness, the Church would have little defence against private versions or distortions of the Gospel. Time and time again the Church has returned to Scripture when its faith has been threatened, not in any spirit of timidity or fear, but as the norm against which other claims to truth are to be tested. This is as true today, with the varieties of sects which come knocking on our doors or accosting us in the streets, as it was in the struggles with the Gnostics in the first Christian centuries. As it has laboured over almost two thousand years to be faithful to the Christ who speaks to us from the Bible, so the Church has developed an understanding of the interpretation of Scripture (*Tradition*), which is still being built up as new issues arise: for example the relationship between theology and the natural sciences, psychology, or modern ideologies, like Marxism.

Many people who accept the place of the New Testament in worship find that the Old presents greater difficulties, because it seems too often to present a God who is blood-thirsty and vengeful, and people whose behaviour matches this. But we need the whole of the Biblical witness, not just the part we find inoffensive, because there is a fundamental unity to it. Even within the Old Testament there is a great difference in the understanding of God shown in Joshua–Judges and in Isaiah 40–55. Much of the language and imagery of the New Testament arises directly out of the Old, as do many of its most central concepts. Two of the most difficult New Testament books, Hebrews and Revelation, cannot begin to be appreciated apart from the sacrificial ritual of the Old Testament or the prophetic and visionary tradition of Ezekiel and Daniel. The New Testament sees itself consistently as the fulfilment of the Old, especially in its expectation of a Messiah. Jesus himself died with the Psalms on his lips. Early attempts to abandon the Old Testament or to edit both (the Marcionite heresy) were resisted. The God of the Old Testament is one and the same as the God and Father of our Lord Jesus Christ. What changes is surely the capacity of his people to receive and to understand his revelation of himself in the coming of his Son.

An expurgation of the most troublesome passages is not even a desirable solution. We need the witness of a book which shows how religion itself can be perverted into oppression and violence. The fact that the Bible does not shirk the violent or the cruel, but witnesses to the power of God to reveal his purpose and his love in the destructive grip of evil, allows us to see in our world, often as horrifying and as productive of despair, that faith can still spring to birth among the ruins of hope. Of this the cross of Christ is the most potent symbol, of both human treachery and divine constancy and triumph. True religion does not flourish where conditions are ideal: it grows among all the crude and base aspects of our existence, and by questioning their hold and their finality looses us from bondage to them and fits us to respond to the values and priorities of Christ.

It is for reasons like these that Christians characteristically speak of the authority and inspiration of Scripture and give to the Bible a place in Christian life which no other text can occupy. It is given us by God and he speaks to us through it, not in any mechanical way but when we are open to him and to the leading of the Spirit, the Interpreter. This does not preserve the Bible from inconsistency or awkwardness, but it does mean that the whole of it witnesses to the searching of God for us and of our searching for him and for the doing of his will. It points to Christ and sets him forth, through the faith of all who went before him and of those few who in the days following his crucifixion and their desertion of him in his dying hour, found themselves empowered against all their expectations to proclaim him as the risen and ascended Lord. The disciples gather fearful in a locked room, and know Christ to be in their midst. Outside, on the road to a nearby village, two others travel home from the city where he was killed and are joined by a third who expounds to them the Scriptures but whom they do not recognise till the breaking of the bread. Already the Church is gathering in faith round the meal of the risen Lord, and the Bible is opening out its witness.

3

LANGUAGE AND THE BIBLE

✠

Colin P. Thompson

"God created man in the beginning in his image and likeness and finally became himself by nature man. Long before
this in his dealings and conversation, as is clearly seen
throughout the Holy Scriptures, it is a wonderful thing to
observe the care the Holy Spirit takes to conform himself to
our ways by remedying our language and imitating all its
variety".

The sixteenth-century Spanish Augustinian who wrote
these words went on to describe how the Bible speaks of joy
and sadness, anger and repentance, threats and blandish-
ments, in fact the whole range of human emotion, so that
we can feel at home with God as he seeks us by his grace.
He saw the Bible and the Incarnation as part of the same
truth. In Incarnation was the climax of a process in which
God had long communicated with his people through
human language. Through the words he had given to his
faithful witnesses, he prepared the way for the Incarnation
of the Word.

We have sometimes been encouraged not to call the Bible
"the word of God", since this is properly the title of Christ,
the pre-existent Logos – "the Word became flesh and dwelt
among us, and we beheld his glory" (John 1.14). Christ is
the truth contained within the whole Bible, and we run the
risk of idolatry if we identify that truth with particular
words from the Bible, especially if we forget that these
words come to us at the end of a long and difficult process
of textual transmission and translation. We can distinguish
"Word" from "word" when we read, but we confuse them

in speech. But the words of the Bible are also God "speaking to us"; they are the first witnesses to his Word. And so we need to pay special attention to its language.

The Bible itself has much to say about language. God and man are shown as conversing with one another in the innocence of Eden, and God brings all the creatures to Adam, "and whatever he called them, that was their name" (Genesis 2.19). One of the consequences of the Fall is the confusion and division created by the loss of a universal language, as the story of the tower of Babel shows (Genesis 11.1–9). In its New Testament reversal, Pentecost (Acts 2) describes how the barriers of communication across many languages were overcome by the one truth of Christ. Changes of name assume importance, because they reveal how individuals respond to the saving work of God: Sarai and Abram become Sarah and Abraham; Saul of Tarsus, Paul. God's word goes forth and does not return to him without accomplishing his purpose (Isaiah 55.11) Jesus names and forces out evil spirits and is himself named by them (Mark 5.1–13) as a sign of his power over the realms of darkness. He "speaks but the word", and healing takes place (Luke 7.7).

The Bible witnesses to the Word through its words; but not through *any* words; they are words of revelation, the words which are given to communicate across times and cultures the meaning of Christ. But in our anxiety to protect the Bible from idolatry, we sometimes go wrong. The words of the Bible are not intended as an obstacle, words to be studied and expounded only by people with degrees in theology; they are intended as revelation, as a means of opening our minds and hearts out to the glory of Christ. The words, metaphors and images in the Bible are given to us to be loved, cherished, cared for; they *matter*; to replace them with other words is to replace a fragment of revelation; to omit them because they are hard to understand is to omit a fragment of the whole.

For the revelation of Christ is not vague or abstract, it is precise, and rooted in human reality. The Word is earthed (Philemon 2.6–8) in the stable, the manger, the Cross, the garden, the mountain, the road to Damascus – because we

14

are earthed, even though our surroundings differ. It may create impact to portray Christ as being born in a shed or executed by a firing squad or appearing to us "not on Gennesaret, but Thames!". But we can make these imaginative transpositions to recreate the meaning of these events in a more vivid or startling way only because they happened as they did. New possibilities spring out of the old events and places; so we bring both old and new out of the treasure (Matthew 13.52).

Yes, you may say, but surely the logical conclusion of this is that we can really appreciate the Bible only in its original languages, and doesn't that mean that only the very clever will be able to respond to it? Careful translation from one language to another is a different matter from imaginative recreation of a past event in modern dress. Arguments about translation have raged for centuries; St. Jerome, who began the influential Latin translation of the Bible from the Hebrew and Greek which came to be called the Vulgate, was no stranger to these. Later, when the Vulgate had reached a position of great authority in the Roman Catholic Church, some scholars fiercely opposed correcting or amending it according to newly discovered manuscripts, and regarded its corrupted Latin texts as infallible. Today, criticisms about new translations still engender great passion.

Words do not correspond exactly in meaning between languages. The Hebrew "shalom" is often said to have a much more comprehensive meaning of well-being and wholeness than our word "peace", its closest translation. But that can be good. We learn directly from the Bible that our own notions of peace need to be revised; that it is not simply the absence of conflict, but includes social justice and the common good. Individuals cannot know true "shalom" if they close their eyes or heart when the hungry starve and weapons of terror are multiplied, because they are implicated in the structures which produce such unease.

A translation should aim at rendering as accurately and as sensitively as possible the meaning of one language into another, but it will always remain a translation, and names

15

and places remain unfamiliar. Although people still argue about the merits of particular translations, no-one seriously disputes the need for the Bible to be translated into different languages. Translation has been a powerful aid to evangelism and education, and since the Second Vatican Council the Roman Catholic Church has been in the forefront of the process, thus ending one of the more fiercely contested issues of the Reformation. A translation of the Bible cannot but produce a combination of familiarity and strangeness. If the translation is to be true to its originals it cannot speak only the familiar language of the moment. For the Bible records the precise experience of many generations of Jews and Christians, and these are part of revelation, not an unnecessary encumbrance. We may listen out for our contemporary prophets because we have read Jeremiah or Amos, though we had better note what they say about true and false prophecy!

The Bible often speaks the universal language of common human experience. Who cannot feel for David as he forgets the majesty of kingship and weeps solitary tears of grief at the death of his rebellious son Absalom (2 Samuel 18.33)? And who cannot at once warm to the father's forgiving love in the parable of the prodigal son (Luke 15.11–32)? Light and darkness, bondage and liberation, waking and sleeping, water and drought, seedtime and harvest, these are images which run through the Bible and through human experience in many cultures and ages. Even so, we can be insensitive to them because our developed technology so often removes them from us – night is banished by electric light, death to the hospital, food appears from all over the world on the shelves of our supermarkets, and water flows from the tap. Conversely, the strangeness of the Bible can become our own language. When black slaves in the Old South sang their songs, they naturally applied the story of the Exodus to their own lives: "When Israel came from Egypt's land, let my people go". They were familiar with the burdens of oppressive labour and with the harshness of alien taskmasters, and they felt themselves to be another Israel in another Egypt, but protected by the same God who had revealed himself so long ago as the liberator of slaves. So too with the non-conformist tradition of giving to Chapels such names as Bethel and Ebenezer. These names were statements about the significance of these places and the people who sought God there. They were buildings which witnessed to the faith of the Bible, set in the midst of buildings which spoke of the wealth of the factory or the slums of the poor; familiar, but strange.

The strangeness is partly to do with the antiquity of the material preserved in the Bible, and its distance from us. The hymn verse "Here I raise mine Ebenezer, Hither by thy help I'm come" nowadays raises a titter rather than speaks from experience. (1 Samuel 7.12) But we can see Palestine, the Sea of Galilee, Capernaum, the Dead Sea, the wilderness of Judea, much more easily today, by travel or on television, than our forefathers could, and our imaginations ought to respond the more readily. The strangeness is not really to do with the names of long-dead people and vanished places, and intellectual archaeology is not its antidote. It belongs to the Gospel itself, which questions so many of our priorities. It tells us that the world's wisdom is foolishness, and that the weakness of a crucified man is the ultimate revelation of the power of God. It calls us to be rich towards God, not rich in things, to interpret notions of power and justice by his revelation of their meaning; and to be reborn according to the likeness of Christ. However familiar the words may sound, there is an underlying strangeness to their meaning and we need to be confronted by them, not let them pass carelessly through the mind. The very reading of the Bible in worship is proclamation, and it needs to be read with awe.

Thus when the great Spanish mystic St. Teresa of Avila used to hear the Bible read in Church in Latin, a language she did not know, she found she sometimes had the gift of understanding what it meant, especially in the beautiful and mysterious love poetry of the Song of Songs. But, writing to her nuns, she advised them not to worry if they failed to understand. Even if the words were translated, she said, they would still be as difficult – if not more difficult – to grasp. What she meant was that even if you understand the words the Bible used, it was another and much more demanding matter to take its message to heart.

The language of the Bible is not our everyday language, which itself will grow old and become the object of study, but the language of a long searching after God and of God's long searching after us, which he "speaks" most completely in the Word made flesh. Its words do not speak out of our culture but from the wisdom and experience of people who stand at the heart of our faith in its most potent revelation. In one sense, all the Bible is translation, for the power of God cannot be exhausted by words, only approached by them. "A sacred reverence checks our songs, and praise sits silent on our tongues". (Isaac Watts). The reality is beyond our grasp, yet "He dwelt among us", and in the Bible Christians find the way prepared for the dwelling and the first voices of those who heard and responded when God spoke in Christ.

The language of the Bible, this translation of the Word into a written yet living tongue, is so rich in images and symbols and so full of bare human experience that we do not need to understand every name or place or allusion. We do not need to know, for example, why it is proper for the author of the Song of Songs to describe human beauty in terms of goats or towers. Because we too can celebrate beauty, and because we too live in a world where its images are manifold, some limited to a time or culture, others common to all, we can respond and be moved. Birth; growth; life; journeying; failure and success; friendship and betrayal; truth and falsehood; goodness and evil; love in life and love beyond death – the Bible takes us to the heart of our humanity and sets in our midst, through many words, the Alpha and Omega, the first and last letters of God's disclosure of himself to us, from the first moment of creation to the consummation of time and history in Christ, the very Word of the Father.

4

SCRIPTURE IN LITURGICAL PERSPECTIVE

✠

Neville Clark

To plot the emergence of the Bible as the Church's Book may be the best way to glimpse the real nature and function of scripture. The point of entry into such an enquiry is to stand with the Church in its early years, survey the landscape it confronted, and watch it come to terms with a tangled inheritance. To assume such a vantage point immediately prompts the asking of one crucial question which otherwise might not obtrude itself as significant.

What were the factors that were to give birth in the fulness of time to the "canon" of the New Testament, a closed collection of writings to which were attributed normative significance? That is the fundamental question. It is a far cry from a body of literature, produced over half a century and more, to the recognition of such writings as sacred scripture vying with the Old Testament in authority. It is an even longer road to that point where all frontiers of entry and exit are closed, the limits of scripture are determined, and a canon is definitively formed. What strange dynamics were at work? And what are the implications for Christian understanding?

One fact at least is clear. The whole concept of a fixed canon of sacred writings is not native to the Christian community in its formative years. Its inheritance from Judaism was the Tradition of Israel, embodied in Law, Prophets, and an open and changing collection of other writings. It did not fall heir to any closed canon. Prior to the final years

of the first century A.D. there was no Jewish canon to
inherit.

The legacy which was available and eagerly appropriated
was the Tradition, its limits flexible, its bounds yet undeter-
mined. The Christian community claimed it for its own,
interpreted it in the light of Christ, and used it with sover-
eign freedom. It was the end of the fourth century before
the Church in general arrived at anything like a fixed Old
Testament canon; and while this included the books we
have been accustomed since the Reformation to call
"apocryphal" it was still a much smaller collection than
that which the writers of the New Testament would themselves have used.

The very existence of the Christian community, however,
meant that alongside the Tradition of Israel a new Tradition was coming to birth. Comparatively early, it began to
find literary expression. By the end of the first century, the
process of collecting the Pauline letters had apparently begun. The Church journeyed into the second century with
most of the writings that were to become the New Testament, but also with other literature that was constantly
added to as the years passed. There was no clearly limited
and universally recognised literary deposit, no "canon",
"standard", or "measuring rod", by reference to which
orthodoxy or heresy might be neatly distinguished. Nor
should this surprise us. The Tradition of the Church was a
growing, living, changing thing, formed in the clashes of
history and the fires of conflict.

By the close of the second century, the shape of the future
was clearly emerging. Though the parallel is by no means
exact, it is broadly true to say that the position of the
Church resembled that of Judaism a century and a half
before. The authoritative Tradition of the Jewish community in the middle of the first century A.D. was Law and
Prophets accompanied by a diverse, shifting, and open-
ended collection of other writings. Similarly, the specifically
Christian Tradition at the beginning of the third century
was embodied in the Gospels and the Pauline letters, allied
to an undefined spread of other literature. Anything like a
fixed canon of the New Testament still lay ahead on the re-

mote horizons. It was the latter part of the fourth century
before the familiar 27 books began to emerge as that New
Testament's generally established and defined content. It
was only in the sixteenth century that the Council of Trent,
provoked by Luther's Reformation, declared the total
canon of scripture closed.

To company with the Church along this tortuous road of
canonical formation is to glimpse again where the beating
heart of her existence lay. It is resided in a living Tradition
which reached back into the dim beginnings of Israel's history and found its transforming fulfilment in Jesus the
Christ. The content and theme of that Tradition was the
redemptive engagement of God with his People. Its unity
rested in the one divine speaking and acting that informed
it. Its power rested in its ability to form and renew a
People's life.

What the Bible presents, then, is a constant divine purpose that has earthed itself in human history, conveyed
itself in human speaking, and brought itself to burning
focus in Jesus. Scripture bears the Tradition of that People
of God whose standing-ground is the place between remembrance and hope. It is a Tradition constantly reformed
because it is always on the way from promise towards fulfilment. Again and again an event or word of promise
announces a fulfilment which will manifest the faithfulness
of God. Yet the fulfilment is never exactly what is expected
and always points on, in promise, to fresh fulfilment. There
is a constant thrust towards an ever-moving horizon. Even
when the future intrudes in final fashion in Jesus, it gener-
ates its own promise and presses forward to what is yet to
be.

But now the question presses. Why then a "canon" of
scripture, bringing the story to a close in the distant past?
Have the divine purpose and activity ceased? Clearly not.
The Church understood herself to be led on still by the
Spirit. Rather is the Bible that part and interpretation of the
ongoing tradition of the People of God – centred on Jesus
Christ, moving towards him and looking back upon him –
in which the Church came to locate that *controlling foundational* story that would thereafter constitute the framework

21

within which all her subsequent story must be inserted and understood.

We have seen that the defining of the authoritative Tradition, the delimiting of the foundational story, was accomplished slowly, painfully, and with some uncertainty. A circle was drawn. But while at the centre the verdict was rendered with confidence, at the circumference there was deep hesitation. The canon of scripture is not so much a smooth and rounded whole as a core with ragged edges. Nor is this surprising. The criteria employed in relation to the New Testament writings might seem a trifle rough and ready. Did a particular book witness to the "orthodox" faith? The question could easily be put, but not as simply answered; for the answer assumed prior agreement on what "orthodoxy" might be. Was a particular book "apostolic"? Here the essential issue was more sharply posed. What was being sought was the assurance that the witness stemmed from the generations standing closest to Jesus. Yet not everything that might be included in that category in fact found place in that canon which was to be the New Testament. And by the time the verdict had to be rendered, the precise origins of some writings were a matter of uncertainty.

Such problems would be disturbing only if the creation of the canon were to be viewed as the erection of a high wall separating absolute light from absolute darkness. The realities of the situation are, however, much more profoundly illumined by a further question that the Church, seeking to discriminate among its literature, found itself posing. Was a book widely and customarily used in the worship of the Christian communities? Such a criterion of judgement was not in itself or on its own in any way decisive. Yet the very nature of the question points to certain significant truths.

The fact is that the Bible is the bearer of a Tradition constantly reforged, reformed, remoulded, reapplied in each new critical situation, each successive age, and that it took shape as the People of God were brought to hear in it and through it the meaning of its existence and the direction of its future. Through the words the Word sounded. In and through the Tradition the presence of God imposed itself in judgement and in mercy. So it is that the setting of certain scriptures at the heart of the liturgical assembly was the obedient recognition that, precisely therein and thereby, the judgement and redemption of God were confronted and the secret of the community's life unveiled.

Nor was this all. For the formation of the canon involved not only the recognition of the customary usage of such scriptures within the liturgical assembly but also the judgement that these writings should, by their continued liturgical use, supremely form and mould the Christian community of the future. The authoritative Tradition was to be unleashed at the heart of the common worship of the People of God, to shape its self-understanding, chart its passage, and control its destiny.

The conclusion is inescapable. The Bible is the authoritative Tradition of the People of God. It belongs essentially at the heart of Christian worship, for it is above all a proclamation to be heard. It is not a handbook of doctrine or ethics. Only in a very indirect way does it provide the controlling context within which the basic decisions of faith and life can and must be made. To it, again and again, must be brought our understanding of God, self, and world, that they may suffer strange deformation and reformation at its hands.

For, in the end, the Church of God and each individual Christian lives with and by scripture in order that formation in Christ may be actualised and continued. We are introduced to an explosive drama, focused in the life, death and resurrection of Jesus, and shaking all human foundations. We are bidden to hear, and hear again, the foundational story which gave us life, shapes the existence of God's People, and will mould the future. But to be engaged by the Bible is to be asked to do more than hear. It is to be called to step on stage, to locate ourselves in the drama, and to allow its story to give us back our identity, form our tomorrows, and thereby become the story of our life.

Such tracing of the foundational story of the People of God inevitably provides the signposts for the right use of the Bible in a Church still travailing in history. To expose the process by which the Story took shape is to do far more than illumine the contours of the restless past. It is to table the agenda for the present. It is to signal perspectives that lay claim to control a sensitive, discerning and fruitful deployment of Scripture in the world of tomorrow.

The urgency of such a challenge is scarcely to be denied. What does it mean to affirm that the Church lives from and by her scriptural charter? What is the creative connection between her storm-tossed originating story and the ongoing tale of the endless years? How does a congregation move to the place where its life is ordered by the Word of God? Where lies obedience, as a perplexed Christian stands before God, with the Bible in his hands?

Everything depends upon the perspective within which such questions are framed. Everything that has been said hitherto presses towards one governing conclusion. The native cradle of scripture is the worshipping life of the People of God. To locate it at any other point is to shut the door to all satisfactory solutions. Its controlling use is its liturgical use. Yet everything here depends upon a true understanding of worship and of the role of the Bible within it. Because the prizes are greatest at this point, it is exactly here that the dangers are most acute. The unleashing of scripture with power stands a hair's-breadth away from its utter domestication, the irretrievable smothering of it in ecclesiastical wrappings, the diverting of it into waters at once smooth and shallow. Upon both minister and congregation is laid a daunting demand.

A congregation is called to an encounter with reality, with all the potential perils and expectant preparedness which that implies. In ancient Israel they had a hunch that the vision of God might mean death. Certainly we live in the era of Jesus Christ, yet there is no guarantee in Christian worship that any man or women will escape unscathed.

Honesty is the supreme requirement. The problem is that set over against that demand is the deep-rooted habit of donning a special religious mask that conceals the real self. This is the mask of piety and virtue. To assume it is to step deftly into an artificial role. Then the face presented to God in worship is spuriously wiped clean of aggression and hate, lust and envy, and Christians conspire together in unholy alliance to offer what they think they ought to be rather than what they are.

Indeed there is often a sense in which the liturgy itself seems to compound the hypocrisy, as it swings to and fro between hymns that commit to unqualified discipleship and prayers that convict of unqualified failure.

It is not surprising if, in such a situation, a seal is placed on the lips of scripture, and its piercing thrust is harmlessly diverted. What if the genuine call to worship is the call to a congregation to become vulnerable, to expose itself in reality and to reality, to lay aside the mask, to be honest with itself and with God! The gathered community may contain Christians who are bored, envious, doubting, lusting, hating, who wish to strike and stab and wound. So be it! Yet once that be admitted, then a congregation is precisely at the Cross, where all men come, where scripture is untethered. For once the real self is unveiled, forgiveness becomes no longer a word but a possibility, healing becomes no longer a remote rumour but a contemporary risk, worship becomes no longer a pretence but an entry upon reality, and the Bible bids fair to become the Word of God.

Nor is this all. Not only must a congregation expose its real self. It must bring the real world with it. Moving towards a purposeful confrontation with the Tradition and the living God who informs it, it may not go unaccompanied by the world of its living. The essential concern of a corporate worship that hinges on scripture is the linking of God's world with God's Kingdom, the setting of all human life beneath the judgement and mercy of the Cross, and under the seal and hope of the Resurrection.

This is why and how the determinative place of the Bible is within the corporate worship of the People of God. This is why and how the liturgical use of scripture is controlling. For worship is rooted in the juxtaposing of the biblical story of the creative, reconciling and redemptive work of God with the variegated and tumultuous life of the world so that a transforming engagement may be effected. The story is the match. The world's life is the material. Worship ignites when the striking of the match sets the raw material ablaze. Combustion cannot occur when Christian men and women hang up human agony and ecstasy on a hook in the church vestibule, to be collected later when spiritual exercises have been completed.

If such is the inescapable scriptural demand with which the Christian congregation is confronted in worship, no less awesome at this point is the responsibility laid upon the minister. Major issues here arise which in the end belong elsewhere, in a discussion of preaching. Yet this much may be said. How the Bible is handled in this decisive context will constitute a most powerful pressure, moulding congregational use and attitude. All the options are open, and therefore all the issues are in the balance. Will the "proclaimer" use scripture as a textbook of doctrine? Will he treat it as an authority for ethics? Will he abstract truth from it? Will he mine from it nuggets of inspiration? Will he simply repeat its utterances in words winged or leaden?

Or will he act as the midwife he is called to be, ushering into the here and now the strange new world of God that wills to disturb and transfigure all human situations? Will he seek to retell the biblical story, to the end that the depths of human living, striving, hoping and despairing are uncovered, familiar ground trembles, and his hearers are challenged to enter or re-enter the vast reaches of the Kingdom?

To erect such governing and delimiting markers in the use of scripture in corporate worship is to follow the pattern of the Tradition itself. Therein, indeed, lies their justification. The biblical spokesmen stand at varying points along the shifting line of Traditions in constant movement. They cannot speak a timeless word, only the word for the hour. They cannot speak from a standing-ground in the past or a cloistered ecclesiastical seclusion in the present, only from the heart of contemporary conflict where God moves to engage his People, and the word must be reborn. They cannot supply the answers to anyone's questions nor the solutions to anyone's problems. They can only stand, themselves and the community to which they belong, between remembrance and hope, launch their God-given story on its transforming mission along the cultural and linguistic rivers of a Canaanite or a Hellenistic world, and so hazard the Tradition for the re-formation in obedience of the People of God. And in the end there is no escape from the "What think ye?" and the "He that hath ears to hear, let him hear".

Hearing indeed, lies at the heart of scripture's liturgical demand. The call is not to read together, or jointly to follow a printed text. It is to hear and receive what once was spoken and heard, and must again be proclaimed in something approaching face to face fashion. This is why there is a basic inappropriateness and misdirection involved in the all too familiar picture of a congregation, eyes down, Bible in hand. Not merely does this tend to diminsh concern for clear, meaningful, proclamatory reading on the part of someone carefully prepared so to do. It also tends to edge the gathered people away from the dynamics of oral speech and the expectations of interpersonal engagement, which properly mark the liturgical drama. This is not the place for a stance more fitted to a bible study group. The urgent offer, clamant demand and transforming promise that constitute scripture's lifeblood, press for the immediacy of the spoken word, and call the hearing ear to a singleminded undivided listening. "Let us *hear* the Word of God" remains the controlling summons.

All this, then, belongs to what may be called the liturgical use of scripture, rooted in the rich context of corporate worship to which it focally belongs. It is only at this point that the question of the so-called "devotional" use of scripture can be faced. That it is introduced at the end, and not at the beginning, is not accidental. It might seem logical to start discussion with the picture of the individual Christian with the Bible in his hand, but the logic of the Gospel points in other directions. Scripture locates itself at the heart of the Christian community and at the centre of its worshipping life. Its liturgical use remains primary. When the community disperses, the Tradition goes with it, to write new commentaries in individual lives.

How then is the Christian to handle the Bible in devotional terms? Essentially he is to let its liturgical use control. He is to allow the perspectives already given to govern his reading, listening and hearing. He is not embarking on some new operation subject to different criteria. He must bring honesty to the biblical encounter, expose himself, be vulnerable, carry his world with him.

Such dealing with scriptures is not to be devoid of controls. There is no licence to switch tracks, as if, in the individual context, a new approach were to become appropriate and an empty mind offer the best key to fruitful engagement with the Tradition. The Christian must come with all the biblical understanding he possesses. That is part of what it means to come honestly, as the man or woman he or she is.

Yet he is not to assume the role of a student. He is not an amateur scholar approaching a defenceless text. He is not burdened with the awful responsibility of deciding what the meaning of the biblical writer might have been. He is not precluded from comprehension or decision until worthy commentators have pointed him in the direction he ought to go. Rather has he been offered the freedom of the biblical city where nothing is won without risks. He may be warned about juvenile foolhardiness; but he cannot really venture nervously clutching an accident insurance policy.

The devotional use of scripture starts – and must start – from the realisation that there is no *one* meaning of the biblical text. The Tradition, formed and re-formed in ever-changing situations and now set over the People of God as authoritative Story, does not and will not speak in one unvarying monotonous tone. No one can predict in advance what it will say to another. Certainly there are dangers. The word that is heard may be the voice not of the Tradition but of personal prejudice, wishful thinking, or desire.

Yet, if there are perils, there are also controls. The Tradition will not contradict itself, in that the word spoken here and now, however new and particular its accent, will always betray a profound and massive identity with the word spoken there and then. So it is that the Christian must listen to scripture as one who comes from the liturgical assembly and moves again towards it, as one who belongs to that People of God which is of yesterday as well as of today.

Given that understanding, the Christian must venture in freedom, take the risk, loose a disciplined imagination upon scripture, and pray through with expectancy what comes to him. Only once more, and for the last time, the goal of that expectancy must be reiterated. The passionate craving for instant relevance and specific direction leads into a cul-de-sac. It is not that there are any absolute boundaries to be set. Faithful and receptive hearing of scripture may indeed resolve a dilemma, prompt immediate action or decision, challenge to specific obedience. To deny that would be to deny Christian experience and bind the Bible falsely.

Yet equally it must be insisted that the normal thrust of scripture is otherwise, and that to hope to have it differently is to court disaster. The Tradition comes not to answer questions, solve problems, or table the specifics of action, but to form and re-form the Christian mind and heart, character and will. The devotional use of the Bible offers no short-cuts to any man or woman. The travail and the uncertainty of plotting the contours of Christian obedience in the tangled paths of living remain, and every valid human resource has to be impressed into service for the discharge of the daunting task.

For the Tradition is – and remains – the Story which wills to become our story and redemptive vision which seeks slowly and painfully to form and inform our lives, the secret of God's tomorrow that aches to become our today. And to live with the scriptural Tradition is to gain the mind-set that belongs to the faithful and obedient People of God.

5

THE ENGLISH BIBLE –
WHICH VERSION FOR WORSHIP?

✠

Gordon S. Wakefield

For 350 years the translation of the Bible published in 1611, which owed much to the initiative and interest of King James I, reigned supreme in the English speaking world. Although popularly known as the Authorised Version, it was never "authorised" in the sense that its use was legally enacted like the *Book of Common Prayer*, but it has been throughout the centuries "the Bible" for English people, the common version so ploughed into our soil that it has borne fruit even in the culture of unbelievers. Its rhythms are, as a whole, incomparable and no rendering has yet replaced it either as "the English Bible" or in liturgical power – though the *Book of Common Prayer* has equalled it in influence, and Coverdale's Psalms, retained there, have bequeathed some haunting lines.[1]

But its language is no longer in common use and makes hard passages and ancient concepts even less intelligible to people today, while scholarship has advanced through the discovery of manuscripts and their comparative study by those with a linguistic equipment far beyond that of Tudor and Stuart times. As early as 1768, John Wesley's *Notes of the New Testament* were appended to an edition of the AV which contained 12,000 alterations.

The official Revised Version of 1881–5 was a conservative project. Yet it is pervasively more accurate and its remarkable fidelity to the original Hebrew and Greek makes it essential for students who have no knowledge of the

Scriptural languages, as Professor H. F. D. Sparks recognised when he chose it for his English *Synopsis of the Gospels*.[2] Its translators adopted the principle of always using the same English word or phrase for the same Greek or Hebrew word or phrase, thus nailing it irremovably to the original, and showing correspondences between books. The invariable use of "straightway" for *euthus* in Mark, is an example of this as well as of the author's limited vocabulary. It should not therefore be undervalued or discarded, and its translators were probably the most distinguished group of Biblical scholars ever assembled. Some later writers, like the Congregationalist, Bernard Lord Manning, disliked it heartily for public reading. But it has some renderings and some have claimed that in Job the solemn splendour "shines through" as it does not through the older version, while in Isaiah 9.1–7 the passage is made intelligible and in Deutero–Isaiah the rhythms are to be preferred.

The problem of the twentieth-century has been that vast increase in scholarship has coincided with the decline of literary English. The language today is by past standards informal, slovenly, undignified, while "ecumenism" both secular and religious has seen the spawning of jargon, often made ugly by a bastard classicism. Both academic expertise and the evangelical desire to present the scriptures in language "understanded of the people" have resulted in a plethora of translations and no Bible – in the sense that there is no one agreed version to teach our children and to read in Church. The individual attempts of many scholars in the first half of the century, most notably the Presbyterian James Moffatt and the Roman Catholic Ronald Knox, have had their day and (almost) ceased to be, though it was said that the latter used to make the choirboys of Winchester Cathedral sit up and listen in the 1950s. The choice is between the American Revised Standard version, cautious and conservative, which with some emendations largely in the interests of Roman Catholic dogma (*The Common Bible*), is being further revised to outlaw both the second person singular in address to God and "sexist" language; the *New English Bible*, monument to the Biblical scholarship of 1945–70, though not intended primarily for reading in Church; the *Jerusalem Bible* (Roman Catholic and recently offered in a new version); the *Good News Bible* (or *Today's English Version*); and the *New International Version*. *The Alternative Service Book of the Church of England* (1980) does not confine itself to any one, but purports to choose the version most suitable liturgically for the set passage.

It is doubtful whether in our time there is any one version which may appropriately sit with authority on the lectern like the chained Bibles of old. There will be several versions in the hands of members of the congregation. And in an age when in theory every voice should be heard and nothing should be imposed from on high, it might be difficult to obtain agreement as to the best. It might even be a matter of so many ears, so many versions, though apparent intelligibility might win most votes with the sense of the numinous second, perhaps a poor second and way behind. Also, as has been noted, the various contenders are undergoing revision and have not reached definitive form, if they ever will, for language is changing with the rapidity of everything else and the archaic may not be the fashion of the distant past so much as of the last decade. Some would contend with a Methodist Faith and Order Study that a plurality of cultures even in one nation may need a plurality of Bible translations as of newspapers.

Some slightly more ample account of the versions currently available in the British Isles may be of help.[3]

1. *The Revised Standard Version*

This is the result of work undertaken by the International Council of Religious Education in which forty major denominations in the United States and Canada were associated. The project was set in hand in 1937, the New Testament was published in 1946 and the complete Bible in 1952. The Apocrypha came later. The aim was "to embody the best results of modern scholarship as to the meaning of the Scriptures, and express this meaning in English diction which is designed for use in public and private worship and preserves those qualities which have given to the King James Version a supreme place in English literature".

English scholars welcomed it and many liturgiologists and leaders of worship would claim that it is the best of the new translations for reading in Church. Occasional Americanisms jar, such as the use of "will" where English demands "shall". Professor Basil Willey thought it unfortunate that the Methodist Church chose it for the prescribed passages in the revision of its service book in preference to the *New English Bible* with which he was involved. It has its infelicities. I Corinthians 13, for instance, has not the rhythm and resonance of 1611. But, understandably, it is the modern version traditionalists prefer.

2. *The Jerusalem Bible* (1966)[4]

The project was inspired by a Roman Catholic Scripture scholar, Father Alexander Jones of Upholland, who was anxious that the notes and commentary of the French *Bible de Jérusalem* (1956) should be available in English, and the best way of doing this would be to attach them to a new English text. A team of translators was selected but Alexander Jones himself, as is the lot of Editors, had to be responsible for no fewer than nineteen books from the two testaments and the Apocrypha. They worked from the French tested by their own knowledge of the Biblical tongues. Anthony Kenny (Jones' nephew, later Master of Balliol) has described the difficulty, in a contentious book like Romans, of avoiding sectarian renderings. He has also told how the poetry of books like Job took over. Like other Roman Catholic translators Alexander Jones found his to be a lonely task which made him suspect to the hierarchy and at times miserable in himself. Like all other translators whatever their denominational allegiance, he had his idiosyncracies and contended for "Yahweh" as the only conceivable rendering of the Divine name in the Old Testament, while other English versions resort to "the Lord". When the *Jerusalem Bible* was approved for liturgical use by the Conferences of Catholic Bishops it was with the proviso that the familiar English name be retained. The *New*

Jerusalem Bible has not been so approved at the time of writing.

3. *The New English Bible*[5]

The aim of this project was to present an accurate and "real" version of the Bible to take an impact on youth and to challenge intelligent churchgoers with its authentic message, "a version which shall be as intelligible to contemporary readers as the original was to its first readers – or as nearly so as possible. It is to be genuinely English in idiom – avoiding equally both archaisms and transient modernisms". As we shall cite below, it has been much criticised by English experts. One Old Testament scholar has written, in a private letter, that it is "marred by the jaded colloquialisms of an earlier generation" (e.g. John 6:60; Acts 24:5). More serious is the confession by a member of the panel that the fundamental questions concerning the text of the OT were not adequately faced. Textual emendation may have been resorted to over-frequently and there has been too much uncritical use of philological conjectures. At present it does not seem able to compete in popularity with the American versions we are about to notice.

4. *The Good News Bible/Today's English Version*

This emanates from the American Bible Society and was strongly promoted by that body and its British counterpart. It is translated according to the principle of "Dynamic Equivalence" for which great claims have been made. Eugene Nida defines it as follows: "To translate is to try to stimulate in the new reader, in the new language the same reaction to the text as the one the original author wished to stimulate in his first and immediate readers".[6] This claims to steer between "formal correspondence" i.e. literalism, and paraphrase, and to produce an effect beyond the mere understanding of the words.

This is not so far removed from the expressed intention of the translators of *NEB*, but it does in fact involve some paraphrase rather than word for word translation and

means that the translation is governed by what the translators believe to have been the original message of Scripture, which can result in tendentiousness and party
interpretation. One notorious instance is Hebrews 9.14
where "His blood will purify our consciences from useless
rituals" is an inaccurate distortion. The English is as far as
possible that of common speech. Slang is avoided but so are
technical terms both ancient and modern which deprive
modern man of entering into Biblical culture and remove
something of Scripture's proper "offence". Long sentences
are broken up, metaphors are changed to similies and
sometimes are removed altogether. So often in difficult passages the translators have taken the easy way out.

With regard to the Old Testament it is specifically stated
that "simplicity and readability were considered more
important than literary quality". The search for modern
equivalents means that Hebrew is deserted and honest
translation abandoned in favour of phrases that appeal to
the perpetrators as "modern". "Anoint", for instance, is
paraphrased by "chosen" (Isaiah 61.1; Luke 4.18); or instead of "You have poured fresh oil over me" (Psalm
92.10), we have "You have blessed me with happiness".
"Girding up the loins" is rendered "dressed for travel"
(Exodus 12.11; cf. Luke 12.35) or "get ready" (2 Kings 9.1;
Jeremiah 1.17) or "prepare for battle" (Nahum 2.1). Isaiah
40 is reduced to casual chit-chat. It is impossible not to
think that, in numerous places, so far from "dynamic equivalence" having been achieved, the impact of the original
has been wantonly lost.

5. *The New International Version*

This is the most recent of the new translations. The whole
Bible was first published in Great Britain in 1979. It is the
work of a transdenominational Protestant group. Accuracy, clarity and literary quality were the aims. It is deliber-
ately designed for public reading and it succeeds in the
poetic books and prophetic oracles of the Old Testament,
though conversations are often rendered colloquially. It is
not always consistent in its modernisations, but its religious

vocabulary will not be strange to the regular churchgoer. It will appeal to the more conservative Churches and church-goers with its attempt to strike a balance between "formal correspondence" and "dynamic equivalence". It has been said that it "is more modern than the *RSV*, less free than the *NEB*, and more literary than the *GNB*".[7]

6. *The Psalms*

Versions of the Psalter deserve separate mention. The *NEB* translators are said to have regarded the Psalms as the most daunting part of their task, as well they might, bearing in mind "the Psalms in Human Life" to quote Prothero's old title, and what a recent philosophic theologian has dis-cerned as the Psalmist's perspective, not of God's existence but of his presence.[8] The *NEB* result cannot be considered altogether happy. The most successful modern version is *The Psalms: a new translation for worship* (Collins 1977) adopted by the Church of England *The Alternative Service Book 1980*. This is superior to *The Revised Psalter* (SPCK 1964). The *Grail* translation (1954–1962) was inspired by the French version of the *Bible de Jérusalem* – a rendering made from the Hebrew. It has had considerable vogue among Roman Catholics – and others – to the Gelineau psalm-tones. As in the French, "special attention was paid to the rhythmic structure of the poetry of the psalms, and this allowed a sung or recited psalmody to be fashioned on the basis of the analogy that exists between the Hebrew tonic rhythm and that of our modern languages".[9]

There should however be some criteria for liturgical read-ing.

(1) *Fidelity to the original*

This depends on well-equipped and ruthlessly honest scholarship. The rendering may often have to be a para-phrase rather than a literal translation and the sentence rather than the individual word will be the unit. As far as possible there must be no bias towards the more recent theologies of which the authors of Scripture knew nothing even though they unwittingly contributed to them. A translator – or a panel – must try to approach a text objectively; this is almost impossible, though the translators of the *Authorised Version* got remarkably near to it for men of their contentious age. Those of us who in our youth benefited from the work and teaching of the dominating directors of the *New English Bible* can perceive in sundry places the influence of their distinctive themes and interpretations, while the *Good News Bible* has been criticised both by Catholic and more liberal scholars, like the late Geoffrey Lampe, because here and there it settles for a rendering which will buttress conservative evangelical theology.

No version can plead entire success at this point; which is why both in private reading and in Church different versions should be in use and should be compared in group study. In this way the lack of a common Bible may be an advantage.

(2) *"Dynamic Equivalence"*

Accompanying the expertise and honesty of scholars, something like this principle should control any translation suitable for congregations.

The aim is most laudable, but it cannot wholly be reached, and has its dangers. Sometimes it gives the modern the advantage at the cost of anachronism, or loss of poetry as when in Genesis I and in the *Good News Bible* "The heavens and the earth" is rendered "the universe", a conception which the ancient world lacked. To strive to create in the men and women of our time something of the excitement and the solemnity with which the message came to the first hearers is a proper task of translators, especially when the version is to be read aloud. But the result may be what in liturgy has been called "representationalism", an attempt to explain and depict too much which fixes the mind on secondary accompaniments, obscures message and mystery alike, and is in the end reductionist and inimical to faith.

(3) *Euphony and the Numinous*

Scripture should sound well. Admittedly some passages have no fine style, no original beauty that we should desire them. The Greek of the Gospels is not elegant and some of Paul's more tortuous arguments needed above all to be put plain, which is where J. B. Phillips succeeded. Nor must Christ's words of judgement be diverted into eloquence.

Though he enthralled his first hearers by his grace it was not always so, and they did not say "Oh! how beautiful", which in any case in our time has sarcastic overtones. Yet William Barclay's remarks that the NT is written in "Daily Express Greek" is unhappily and, for a scholar, curiously misleading.

And Hans Urs von Balthasar has argued that the needs of our world must enhance beauty in the eternal triad of beauty, truth and goodness:

In a world without beauty – even if people cannot dispense with the word and constantly have it on the tip of their tongues in order to abuse it – in a world which is perhaps not wholly without beauty, but which can no longer see it or reckon with it; in such a world the good also loses its attractions, the self-evidence of why it must be carried out – In a world that no longer has enough confidence in itself to affirm the beautiful, the proofs of the truth have lost their cogency. In other words, syllogisms may still dutifully chatter away like rotary presses or computers which infallibly spew out an exact number of answers by the minute. But the logic of these answers is itself a mechanism which no longer captivates anyone. The very conclusions are no longer conclusive. And if this is how transcendentals fare because one of them has been banished, what will happen with Being itself? – Will this light (of Being) not necessarily die out where the very language of light has been forgotten and the Mystery of Being is no longer allowed to express itself? What remains is then a mere lump of existence which, even if it claims for itself the freedom proper to spirits, nevertheless remains totally dark and incomprehensible even to itself. The witness borne by Being becomes untrustworthy for the person who can no longer read the language of beauty.[10]

Those literary critics who have deplored modern versions of the Scriptures have often been shrill and cantankerous and seem to have spoken for a cultural élite, often agnostic, rather than for humble believers or those who are in search of Christian understanding; but they cannot be ignored when a public Bible is required to be read in the congregation and before the world. Nor can such a Bible be content with going back to the original, not only because in many places that is impossible to recover, but also because use throughout the centuries has gathered to the text associations which have themselves become sacred and which it is impious to shatter at a stroke.

T. S. Eliot, who was a Churchman, wrote that the *New English Bible* is something "which astonishes in its combination of the vulgar, the trivial and the pedantic". If it were only for private reading "it would be merely a symptom of the decay of the English language in the middle of the twentieth-century. But the more it is adopted for religious services the more it will become an active agent of decadence."[11]

That is harsh; but it is the judgement of what Frank Kermode has in another context called the "circumcised ear"; this time of the poet.[12] The *NEB* has some noble passages (e.g. Hebrews 12.18 ff). But in modern renderings banality seems forever lurking at the door; and the more revisions chase the phantom of colloquialism and are stampeded by the screams of pressure-groups, the more reductionist they will become. There are instances in the *New Jerusalem Bible* to illustrate that. A *Guardian* article hardly escapes the charge of journalistic lampoon, a making ridiculous by selection of especially unfortunate renderings; but the Editor of the *Expository Times*, Dr Cyril Rodd, finds some solecisms, and exposes the threat to honesty, and historical understanding and downright distortion, of trying to render in "non-sexist" language texts which derive from a society in which women *were* subordinate. To pretend that the Old Testament is a late twentieth-century work, is a gross falsehood and ignores the historical nature of the Christian revelation. Dr Rodd welcomes *NJB* as a study Bible but is not sure how it will be received when used in worship.[13]

Ian Robinson in a savage, though learned and powerful attack, considered *NEB* to have been "an essay in nice, polite, donnish journalese" which cheapens the mystery of the Gospel and makes the New Testament propaganda for the atheist. "The *NEB* miracles all seem gross impostures, superstitions as reported by the modern journalist".[14] There is this danger in modern translations, though some would welcome it as doing justice to the belief that the Christian's is the "everyday God", not only or chiefly "the high and holy one that inhabiteth eternity". There is room for debate here. Yet Robinson is right to claim that neither the Bible nor the Christian faith are here to make life *easier* for us. There is mystery, and that which is a scandal to plainness and perspicuity as well as what is hidden from the wise and revealed to babes. As Pascal declared "Say what you will there is something astonishing about the Christian religion".[15] And this is to be experienced by the reading of Scripture in Church.

(4) *Folk Memory*

We have already touched on this. "Suffolk farm-workers still use the incomparable English of the *Book of Common Prayer* and the *King James Bible* with naturalness and ease". So Ronald Blythe in *Akenfield*.[16] The retort is easy – the multi-cultural populations of our conurbations have few links with rural England; a Bible translated in 1611 cannot speak to youth brought up on television. Yet do newer versions have any more meaning for these? What may make understanding easier for believers may be irrelevant to elemental human need which craves less for words than for rituals, symbols, and sounds which console as they reach back to the past and represent the unchanging. This may be as true for leather-jacketed groups of motor-cyclists as for sorrowing old women or intellectuals on occasional visits to worship. The most damaging critique of the new translations could be that they are "pleasantly unmemorable".

How is a Church to decide on a version for its staple usage?

There are two possibilities:

(a) To adopt the method of *The Alternative Service Book 1980* and to choose from the various translations that version of the set passage which seems most suitable.

If so, the *Authorised Version* should not be discarded. It cannot be bettered for the Creation story in Genesis I, or the sacrifice of Isaac (Genesis 22) or the Lucan birth narratives or some of the sayings of Jesus. Some of the individual translations we have noted in passing have their linguistic triumphs and should not be ignored. Ronald Knox's fortieth of Isaiah is an instance.

Church of England congregations are becoming used to this method in the Eucharistic lections. For other public readings it would require either reliance on the judgement of the Minister or hard work by a representative group of the congregation which in larger churches should not be difficult to assemble. It ought to include one person with some knowledge of the Biblical languages (presumably the Minister), one person who teaches English, as well as people who have a good and practical (if not a trained) ear and an instinctive "feel" for what aids not only understanding but worship.

Yet this fails to provide a common Bible, which is essential if there is to be a grasp of Scripture as a whole and not merely of liturgical snippets; essential, too, if memory is to be stored, if the Bible is to furnish the language of prayer. Otherwise, Christianity will not only be lost from our language and much of our culture; it will be captured by those heresies which have assailed it from earliest times and against which Scripture has been a safeguard since the end of the second century. Thus the second possibility must be urged:

(b) One of the modern versions must become the Bible most in use. As has been mentioned, the *Good News Bible* has gained much ground and it is rumoured that within a few years it will be a permitted text for public examinations.

We cannot but feel that this would be injurious both to literature and to faith.

Admittedly a perfect version does not exist and this we must accept. In the Roman Catholic Church the *Jerusalem Bible* has emerged as the version read in the overwhelming majority of congregations.

The *RSV* continues to find favour among liturgiologists – witness the JLG *Holy Week Services* (1983) and the Church of England *Lent, Holy Week and Easter Services* (1986) where the Passion Narratives are all from *RSV*, and half of the Vigil Lessons also.

This is the translation to which we would give priority. We hope that revision will not make it less liturgically acceptable. And in spite of all the criticisms and the original disclaimers, the *New English Bible* has proved acceptable for public reading, far and wide, and is usually accurate. A revision could improve it, especially if it not only heeds the strictures of good writers and poets, but faces the fundamental questions about the Old Testament text. A Church could do far worse than have *NEB* on its lectern.

Sometimes mediocre and inadequate versions may be redeemed by good reading. Like the choice of version, the office of reader is one which requires care. Readers should constitute an order as in the ancient Church; and neither be members of the congregation taking it in turns, nor half-rehearsed children. It will be made plain in this book that the public reading of Scripture is as much as preaching, the ministry of the Word. It is the proclamation of Christ through sense and sound, "the old, old story" which confronts our tired humanity with the music of the gospels and the beauty which is ever new. It carries us back to the beginning when the morning stars sang together and all the sons of God shouted for joy, onward through all the tribulations and achievements of history to the Cross where time and eternity meet, and makes us hear distant echoes of the triumph song of heaven.

This chapter owes much to help received from Revd Canon Professor Douglas R. Jones and the Revd Professor Emeritus G. W. Anderson.

NOTES

1 See W. D. Maxwell, *The Book of Common Prayer and the Worship of Late Non-Anglican Churches* (Friends of Dr Williams Library, Third Annual Lecture, 1950) Stella Brook, *The Language of the Book of Common Prayer*, 1965.

2 H. F. D. Sparks, *A Synopsis of the Gospels*, 1964. See also his Ethel M. Wood lecture, *On Translations of the Bible*, 1973. C.f. A. T. Quiller-Couch, *The Art of Writing*, 1916.

3 For full accounts and assessments see F. F. Bruce, *The English Bible*, 2nd ed. 1970, A. C. Partridge, *English Bible Translations*, 1973, Sakae Kubo and Walter F. Specht, *So Many Versions?* Revised and Enlarged ed., Zondervan, 1983.

4 There is a fascinating account of the work of this translation in Anthony Kenny, *A Path from Rome*, 1985, Chapter IX, pp. 113–123.

5 In addition to works listed in n. 3, see Geoffrey Hunt, *About the New English Bible*, 1970 and Denis Nineham (ed.) *The New English Bible Reviewed*, 1965.

6 Eugene Nida, *The Theory and Practice of Translation*, 1969, p. 29.

7 Kubo and Specht, op. cit., p. 272.

8 J. Kellenberger, *The Cognitivity of Religion: Three Perspectives*, 1985. C.f. Rowland E. Prothero (Lord Ernle), *The Psalms in Human Life*, 4th ed., 1913.

9 J. Gelineau, Introduction to *The Psalms: a New Translation from the Hebrew arranged for singing to the Psalmody of Joseph Gelineau*, 1967, p. 10.

10 Hans Urs von Balthasar, *The Glory of the Lord. A Theological Aesthetics I*, 1982, p. 14.

11 T. S. Eliot, *The Sunday Telegraph*, 16th December 1962, reproduced Denis Nineham, op. cit., pp. 100–101.

12 Frank Kermode, *The Genesis of Secrecy*, Harvard 1979, p. 16.

13 *The Expository Times*, vol. 97, no. 4, January 1986, p. 100 ff.

14 Ian Robinson, *The Survival of English*, 1973, p. 22 ff.

15 E.g. *The Thoughts of Blaise Pascal*, translated from the text of M. Auguste Molinier by C. Kegan Paul, 1899, p. 186. The french is "on a beau dire, il faut avouer que la religion chrétienne a quelque chose d'etonnant". The translation I have used is that of R. W. Church, *Pascal and Other Sermons*, 1896, p. 20.

16 Ronald Blythe, *Akenfield: Portrait of an English Village*, 1969, p. 58.

6

READING THE SCRIPTURES IN PUBLIC

— ✠ —

Donald McIllhagga

In the two-way "conversation" which is worship, if the proclamation of the Word is to be effective, then *how* it is read matters. God, in speaking to his people, needs a human being, or human beings, whom he uses sacramentally so that his Word can be heard. This being so, we must give high importance to the way the Scriptures are presented in worship.

Attention

In our "TV" world we have the real problem of gaining attention. In our largely non-verbal world we are about to ask a congregation to respond to a largely verbal communication. We must enable their listening, for "faith comes by hearing" (Romans 10.17). If the act of listening embraces every faculty a hearer possesses, as indeed it should, care must be taken on the part of those who read, first to gain attention.

This will involve two things; making sure the "setting" is right, and then introducing the reading in the best possible way.

Concerning the setting

First there are a number of possible "eye-gate" accompaniments which will help to open the "ear-gate". The copy of the Bible which is read can "come into focus" by being carried to the place where it is to be read. This may happen in a Reformed Church where at the beginning of the service the Bible was carried in, perhaps by the person who is later to read, and placed open on the Communion table. Now it needs to be taken to a lectern or pulpit. This should be well lit and on a higher level than the congregational seating, so the reader is fully visible to everyone. If the reading desk is adjustable it should be at such a height that a reader's face can be seen, rather than the top of the head. If there is no lectern and the book has to be held, the same "rules" apply. Ideally the reading should take place in the same position from which the sermon will be preached so that a unity of visual focus is established.

Second there is the question of how a reading is to be introduced. Unless it is printed on an order of service the reference to the part of the Bible from which it is taken will have to be given. "The first reading is Isaiah, chapter 63, the sixth verse". The word "first" could be "Old Testament". The second or subsequent reading might be "Epistle" or "Gospel". Although some traditions would emphasise that the word "comes alive" best simply by it being read and heard, nevertheless one reason why the reference should be given is that some people will wish to follow the lesson in their own Bibles – even if the reading is in a different version; in the belief that what we hear and see we "take in" better than what we hear only. However, to limit the introduction to these bare facts is perhaps rather "clinical" and two other things may be done. The first, common in the Church of Scotland and some of the English Free Churches, is to precede the facts by "Hear the Word of God (as it is contained) in . . .". This however raises a theological question for some. Is not the Word of God a living Word in some greater sense than the sum of the words written in this passage? And does not such an announcement presume a fundamentalist view about the inspiration of scripture that it is unfair to impose on the hearers? Some readers avoid this problem and at the same time add to the "getting attention" by announcing the reference and then adding "(We) Listen for the Word of God". A different view may be

45

taken of the concluding phrase "This is the Word of the Lord" said after a lesson has been read, as suggested by (e.g.) the *Alternative Service Book* of the Church of England, and especially if the phrase is used after rather than before a silence following the reading. One must presume that the Holy Spirit has acted to make the words a living Word.

A number of volumes of Prefaces or Introductions to lessons, each associated with a particular lectionary, are published. Such prefaces should be brief, simple, concise. They can however be useful, for example to show the link between the lessons. Also if they are faithful summaries of the text they can suggest to people what they should listen for in the actual reading.

There is something in the advice "Tell them what you're going to tell them (preface), then tell them (reading), then tell them what you've told them (sermon)". Such introductions should be written out to ensure accuracy and brevity.

There are two "editing" points which can usefully be added here. If there are personal pronouns at the beginning of a passage, "He said to him", it will be very difficult for listeners to pick up who is speaking to whom. Simply substitute the (right) names. Similarly "Go there and return here" – substitute the place names. There may be an "and" (or other unnecessary conjunction) at the beginning of the passage, which can be dropped. Also omitting some verses from a passage can help the sense, though if this kind of editing is going to be done, announce the fact, and of course check first with the preacher!

The Readings

The reader may or may not be responsible for selecting them, for deciding on their number and for deciding on which version to use. These are however all important matters, not least as they relate to their "performance".

Although normally two or three readings would be expected, if only one reading is used it may be easier to keep in mind as the service moves on to the sermon, and if a reading is necessarily long the general balance of the service may be helped by having only one. This one should relate to the season or the worship theme (see the "controlling" Lection in the Lectionary of the Joint Liturgical Group). If there are two lessons they should probably be from Old and New Testaments to demonstrate the fulfilment of the former by the latter. If there are two New Testament lessons, Epistle and Gospel, a certain comprehensiveness is achieved, with reference to the life of Israel, the life of the early Church, and the life of Jesus.[1] As it is difficult for people to keep attention, lessons should normally not be too long, though the sense, especially in narrative passages, will determine the length in practice.

It is generally accepted today that with the occasional exception such as the use of the Authorised Version at a funeral or a Christmas service of "Nine Lessons" a modern version should be read both for the sake of accuracy and for the sake of "keeping attention". The best version of a particular passage will be a question of individual judgement, and no doubt the general "feel" of a translation will be taken into account. However the decision must be made, and may be the responsibility of the reader. The simplest thing to do is to read through several versions and decide which can be read aloud with most meaning. The Church of England's *Alternative Service Book* selects what it considers to be the best translation for reading aloud, and uses the *Revised Standard Version, Today's English Version*, the *New English Bible* and the *Jerusalem Bible*.

The use of paraphrases of scripture rather than translations such as those by Barclay,[2] Dale,[3] or Phillips,[4] or indeed the use of paraphrase hymnody ("While shepherds watched" etc. or metrical psalmody) is more problematical. Such paraphrases may however supplement and occasionally substitute for passages with great benefit to a congregation. Whether readings should be added which are not scriptural is another question. If they are, they should be a "fourth lesson" and not replace the scriptures.

Audio-Visual Aids

Some accompaniments to the reading of scripture which

help to make that reading a "high point" have already been mentioned, e.g., the carrying of the Bible, the "Little Entry" in the Orthodox tradition. Another is standing for the reading, most commonly the Gospel – but not necessarily the Gospel.

Another is to light a candle to symbolise the Word of God being "a lamp to our feet, a light to our path", as might be done on the Second Sunday of Advent, often called Bible Sunday.

In some traditions, particularly the Anglican and the Roman Catholic, the reading of the Gospel is always the high point in the 'Liturgy of the Word' and certain words and actions emphasise this. When the Gospel book is carried to the lectern it is "preceded by servers with candles and incense or other symbols of reverence ... (the reader) bowing in front of the one presiding, asks and receives a blessing ... At the lectern the one who proclaims the gospel greets the people, who are standing (to show honour), and announces the reading as he makes the sign of the cross on forehead, mouth and breast. If incense is used, he next incenses the book, then reads the gospel. When finished, he kisses the book ... (and) it is appropriate for introductory and concluding words to be sung ... a way both of bringing out the importance of the gospel reading and of stirring up the faith of those who hear it".[5] We must note however that there is a variety of practice in different traditions. The Calvinists of the 18th Century stood for all lessons, as indeed the Lutherans have always done to give equal honour to all parts of scripture, and no doubt those who treat all lessons the same today, whether they stand or sit, would give the same reason now.

In addition to the ceremonial, there are other "Audio-Visual aids" that might be used. Pauline M. Webb tells of an ecumenical occasion when an African drummer dramatically beat out introductions to a series of passages beginning with the word "Today". She tells how another visual impact came unexpectedly when four people read four of the Gospel stories relating to people they themselves resembled (Simeon, Anna, Zacchaeus, and the women who anointed Jesus' feet).[6]

Other examples come from the *Holy Week Services* of the Joint Liturgical Group[7] where the Maundy Thursday service provides for the washing of feet in association with John 13.1–15, and the Palm Sunday and Good Friday Services provide for the dramatic reading of the Passion Narratives by three people. The extension of this would be to dramatise a passage of scripture, or to use groups of voices, say in the reading of a psalm.

The Reader

A reader inevitably interprets a passage for those who listen. This is done by the use of the voice and the body. They are the instruments God is using to "play his tune".

Both the production of the voice and its emphasis are important. The most frequently-given advice to speakers in any circumstances is "Speak *up* and speak *out*", and this is sound advice. An adequate sound is produced if the mouth and chest are used as resonating chambers. There is a good summary in a United Reform Church preaching leaflet,[8] "Open your mouth when you speak ... Try to look at the congregation as you speak. Don't chop your voice at the end of sentences, and be careful to enunciate consonants at the end of words. ... In a church which you are visiting for the first time it's a good idea to try out your voice ... when you arrive. But remember that the acoustics of an empty church are very different from those of a full one."

As Richard G. Jones points out[9] "in small churches there is a great temptation to relax into a conversational style – almost always wrong. In medium-sized buildings there is no alternative but constantly to throw the voice to the back of the church (where deaf people usually sit). In large churches there is probably a microphone and the technique is totally different. You need to stand in front of it and not to stray too far on either side, then to speak clearly as if in a large room. The clarity of the speech will matter much more than the volume, and if you want to woo the congregation with a strong whisper let it be from very close indeed to the microphone and then when the speech level is returning to normal, stand back again ... (and) Do not sing loudly into it!"

49

The way one breathes is the clue to confident speech. Before beginning, a deep breath through both mouth and nose will help, as will continuing to breathe deeply but naturally. It is possible to make a determined effort to relax, especially the throat and shoulders, and this is helped, as is a full speaking tone, by standing on both feet securely in contact with the floor.

The *emphasis* we give to our speech depends on five factors: pitch, pace, pausing, inflexion and tone. The *pitch* can be varied to suggest excitement, activity, awe, reflection, peace, serenity. Simply raising or lowering the voice adds interest, and the opposite, a monotone, is boring. The decision to vary pitch does of course exclude the possibility of "intoning" scripture in an attempt not to impose any human influence and allow the text to "speak for itself". We are making the assumption that God uses the "personalising" of a reading to convey more meaning than could otherwise be done.

The *pause* can be used to emphasise and to heighten dramatic effect. It is essential before an announcement. It sets up the hearer's expectancy for what will follow. A good example for practice is John 20.24–29. Generally, subordinate words such as articles and conjunctions should be under-emphasised unless it is necessary to "punch" them for a specific meaning, a rule not always followed by radio announcers these days. The pause will also make for clarity. It will enable the word following to be heard better. A long pause becomes a silence, which can be very appropriate at the end of a reading *before* any concluding words are used, such as "This is the Word of the Lord" or "The Lord bless to us this reading from his Word".

Pausing relates to *pace*. Again, speed will reflect the content of what is being said. Slowing down may emphasise a new, important idea; rapid speech could show a defensive or urgent reaction like Philip's "Lord, show us the Father and we shall be satisfied", or Peter's "You shall never wash my feet". Generally the pace needs to be slower in church than in normal conversation, to compensate for the size of the building.

Inflexion and stress in the voice can help listeners by

reflecting mood, suggesting questions, implying amusement, joy, sadness, sarcasm, irony, approval and disapproval. And the overall *tone* of the voice, though at times it may have to be sharp (e.g. as it rebukes God) or gentle (e.g. in the exchanges between Ruth and Naomi), needs to be dignified though certainly not pompous or stiff. It needs to be warm, without being casual or conveying a false heartiness.

All these matters concerning the voice are important, though none of them needs to be overdone. The reader is not projecting himself or herself as in a dramatic recitation, but is always a servant of the Word of God. May it be said of us what was said of Dietrich Bonhoeffer, "He read as if he were listening..."

A final word on the voice may be added about *accent*. Although one has to be aware of the "lazy" accent, like that of the Southern States of the USA, there is never need to be ashamed of a regional accent – such are part of the varied richness of the English tongue. Just as slovenly speech is "out", so is the artificial "pulpit voice" and an attempt to "talk posh". One's natural speech is what is required. In all these matters one honest critic (sitting in the back pew) is far more helpful than all the words that can be written in a book. Any major fault that is discovered can probably be ironed out with ease by a drama teacher, an elocutionist or perhaps a speech therapist.

Incidentally, if during a reading you make a mistake, as all readers do from time to time, do not confound it with "sorry" or "oops", a nervous laugh, or by making a face. Simply repeat the word or phrase or sentence and continue as though nothing had happened. If you don't call attention to the mishap it probably will go unnoticed.

Not only the voice but the reader's "body language" will be part of the interpretation of the passage being read, and the aspects of this we need to consider briefly are posture, dress and movement. You will give some thought to what you should wear. The keynote will be "modesty" rather than "flamboyance", though these days there are really no "rules" in this matter. Clearly some liturgical occasions are more formal than others, and this may be reflected in the use of vestments, both lay and clerical.

All movement will be discreet, as befits a servant. Your "entrance" should not be a last moment rush, perhaps creating anxiety that it is not known what is to happen next. If the reading is preceded by music or a corporate act (like the recitation of a psalm or an alleluia) move before it is concluded. If a prayer, then move as soon as the "Amen" has been said. If you are physically able, stand straight and walk with poise calmly and quietly. If you are not, do not worry, your inner calm and poise will still "come over". Stand still. Avoid shifting awkwardly from side to side. Put your hands gently on the desk of the lectern, for this will enable you unobtrusively to place a finger at the margin of the text. Thus, if you have occasion to look away from it, you will easily find your place again.

Don't "look up" after each sentence, as if seeking approval for what you are doing, but do feel free to make eye-contact with the congregation when you think that would have some significance – when a new paragraph starts, when the text switches from general principles to its application to ourselves, when a question is being directed to those listening, etc. Occasionally looking at people reminds them that you are reading to them. Like your "entrance", your "exit" will be without fuss. After pausing and then saying "This is the Word of the Lord", or whatever conclusion is called for on the occasion, you will return to your seat chosen on this day close to the lectern.

If you realise that the living Word of God is using you as his "instrument", then you will feel alive and look alive. You will find that you are in control of the situation from beginning to end. You will of course be most fully in control if you have taken the trouble to understand and to prepare what you are to read.

Your understanding will relate to the type of literature that you are to read, for there is great variety in the Bible – narrative, ethical treatise, poetry, prophecy, apocalypse, letters, laws, and other forms. Your understanding will "make your own" what you are to proclaim to others. Your preparation will help you to decide how you will read. The result will be no less than a sharing in the action of God who through Christ reveals his saving truth. You will be

playing your small but significant part in the task of proclaiming the good news of our redemption, and in the
building up of the Body of Christ.

NOTES

1 Neil Dixon, *Approach with Joy*, p. 11.
2 W. Barclay, *Daily Study Bible* &c.
3 A. Dale, *Winding Quest* and *New World*.
4 J. B. Phillips, *New Testament*.
5 Introduction to *The New Sunday Missal*, para. 17.
6 Pauline M. Webb, *Eventful Worship*, p. 20 f.
7 Donald Gray, ed., *Holy Week Services*, 1983.
8 *Speaking and Reading in Church*, Lay Preaching Matters, Leaflet 11.
9 Richard G. Jones, *Groundwork of Worship and Preaching*, p. 221.

7

OF TIME, CALENDARS AND LECTIONARIES

✠

Gianfranco Tellini

What is time? A medieval philosopher would have offered a definition with a marked degree of confidence: "time is the duration or permanence in being of any created reality, however much this reality may in itself be subject to change".

A contemporary scientist could not answer the same question with anything like the confidence of the medieval philosopher. The discovery of quantum mechanics has led some physicists to call into question both the nature of time and the very nature of reality. Why this should be so need not concern us here: suffice it to say that in following the methods characteristic of their discipline, physical scientists have rediscovered in recent times an insight into the Jewish-Christian religious tradition which many a Christian theologian had long forgotten, namely that the question of the meaning of time is indissolubly linked with the question of the meaning of reality itself.

Defining time is no easy thing. Fortunately for us, we need not attempt to do so here. It is enough for us to describe the way in which time is experienced through the direct evidence of our senses. Our experience of time is that of an objective, irreversible and uninterrupted process of coming to be and passing away whereby the future becomes the present and is instantly already the past. No effort of ours, except in fantasy or wishful thinking can stop its flow, make the past become the present, or cause the future to

54

hasten or delay its coming. Our experience of time is not far from what the Aristotelian philosophers of the Middle Ages taught when they tried to define the very essence of time as "that dimension of the universe whereby the duration or permanence in being of things and events can be measured in a uniform way".

The most obvious way of measuring the flow of time is by means of the cycles of Nature. The alternation of light and darkness gives us the day as a first unit of measurement. The phases of the moon and the alternation of the seasons give us the most elementary form of two further units: the month and the year. With the improvement of technology and the increasing sophistication of our social life, these three units are constantly redimensioned and refined. We now have quartz watches and atomic clocks, Greenwich mean time and twenty-four time zones, local mean time and local summer time. Nature provides us also with many other such "clocks", including the bio-rhythms of the human organism. Our physical and mental well-being demand that these various "clocks" be harmonised as far as possible in a well-ordered pattern of existence. Hence the necessity of applying this kind of knowledge to such apparently unrelated subjects as liturgical time and liturgical calendars.

We measure time, and in so doing find that we are measured by it. We experience ourselves as an integral part of the very irreversible process we observe and so the question of time becomes inextricably linked with the question of meaning: what, if any, is the meaning of our being and of our becoming? Almost imperceptibly, the category of "objective time" slides into the category of "human time", or time with human meaning. Who am I? How do I relate to what is? What is the meaning and purpose of it all? This quality of time is determined by its content in realtion to us: by human actions, setbacks, desires and expectations. As a consequence, psychological balance depends to a great extent on our having a positive attitude to our past, on our acceptance of the present and on the quality of our future expectations: time and meaning go together.

In our direct experience, time is structured in cycles and

appears to follow a pattern of "eternal return". At the level of the single event it is change (the change from being to non-being, from birth to growth, decay and eventually death), but at the level of the whole it appears to be a continuous line curved into an endlessly repeatable circular pattern, so that, as Ecclesiastes noted, nothing is new under the sun. Does history obey a law of eternal return or a law of ultimate purpose and design? We must choose. For the believer the consequences of such choice are many and far reaching.

If, on the one hand, history obeys a law of eternal return, the ultimate meaning of the existence of all things is the result of a divine intervention, or hierophany, revealing the original pattern of everything, that is, the way in which things were "in the beginning" and God, or the gods, willing, they will always be. The changing world of human historical time would then be the world of the profane, a world infinitely distant from the changeless dimension of the sacred. The chasm between the sacred and the profane would be bridged only by means of "sacred rites" revealed by the gods themselves and therefore to be performed according to absolute, indispensable and unchangeable rules. Through the performance of the sacred rites according to such rules by persons specifically chosen by the gods, the benefits of the original hierophany would be made present in the here-and-now: the purpose of the sacred rites would therefore be that of transforming mere remembrance into "anamnesis". The cosmic phenomenon would have been the the exclusive medium of the original revelation. We would speak therefore of two kinds of "sacred time": mythical sacred time (the time in which the hierophany took place) and ritual sacred time (the time occupied by the sacred rite). Through the correct performance of the rite, the sacred quality of time originating from the mythologisation of the cosmic phenomenon would be made to extend to the time of the rite. Properly celebrated, the rite would ensure that things would continue the way they had always been and human beings would find themselves in total harmony with both the divine and the original meaning and purpose of the world. If history followed such a law of "eternal return", there could be no real eschatology, no heavenly design to bring together the human and the divine. On no account could we hope that one day things might be better, let alone see the human race as the chosen instrument of that coming-to-be.

On the other hand, history could be thought to follow a law of purpose and design. Within the apparent eternal return of the natural cycles, the eyes of the believer would be made to perceive, through grace, the action of God. The flow of time would then appear as a purposive, continuous and open line moving from an Alpha to an Omega, from a beginning to an end. The revealed meaning of the universe would be determined not by its beginning, but by its future complete fulfilment. To find one's place within the general scheme of things and therefore to derive meaning for one's existence, one would have to respond positively to God's enabling call and become of one's free-will the living instrument of his purpose. The ceremonies of worship would be one of the many possible instruments of dialogue between God and his people and one of the many possible moments in which the divine imperative is re-proposed (and divine power given) to carry out God's will faithfully and efficiently.

In this paper, we are concerned with the answer to three questions. Is there a specifically Christian understanding of time? How may a Christian be expected to experience it? Should the specifically Christian experience of time be made to lie at the heart of the visible structure of Christian liturgical calendars and lectionaries?

The answer to the question of the nature of time comes no more easily to a contemporary Christian theologian than to a modern philosopher. The biblical writers were not given to speculation of the abstract kind. Their purpose was not to provide us with an encyclopedia of theology, but with a statement of their experience of the living God. The history and tradition of the Church offer us plentiful, but doubtful, material: at any given time, we cannot help being influenced to a greater or lesser extent by the transitory cultural values of the world in which we live. Many of our values are often determined not by theology, but by the circumstances of the age. They are often taken for granted and challenged only from time to time as the circumstances change. The best we can do in trying to answer this question is to interrogate the Bible indirectly by referring to two related themes spoken about extensively in both the Old and the New Testament: the themes of creation and of the ultimate purpose of God.

Differing in this from the holy books of other religions, the Bible is not greatly interested in the question of the origins of the world. Creation is seen as the starting point of the execution in time of the purpose and design of a God who is Other and yet all-near and caring. God's original creative act marks the absolute beginning of time: time is itself the creation of God. Before time began, God was. What time is for God we cannot say: his existence transcends our measure and imagination. Time, as we experience it, is the framework within which God, the Creator of a world which has not yet found its ultimate fulfilment, unfolds his design. It is the framework of a history which concerns us both ultimately and directly.

The very notion of "beginning" implies an "end" as well as a "final purpose". It implies also a "process in time" within which this purpose is achieved. God's purpose in creating the world is revealed as one of "salvation": a condition of total fulfilment, a state of unity and harmony between Creator and creature, involving both us and the cosmos (Isaiah 65.17; 66.22–23); 2 Corinthians 5.17–19; Ephesians 1.9–10; 3.1–12; Colossians 1.20). The special kind of history of which the act of creation is the starting point is therefore a "history of salvation".

God's creative power and his Lordship of history must be seen as correlative. All creatures receive from him both their being and their destiny. The overall flow of history is given its direction by means of a succession of events (in the Greek, *kairoi*), which are both further revelation and further actualisation of God's purpose. In a sense it may be said that God creates such specific, significant events (Isaiah 48.1–7; Judith 9.5–6). Not all events are equally significant in this respect. What remains constant in this fleeting world is the hope to which we are called. Ultimate meaning is given to an event solely by its relation to God's ultimate purpose.

The original act of creation took place through the Word, God the Father being both the *terminus a quo* and the *terminus ad quem* of the creative process and therefore also of the process of history (Wisdom 8.6; 9.9; John 1.3; 1 Corinthians 8.6): as the Shorter Catechism puts it, we were created "to glorify God and enjoy him for ever".

The Word through whom all things are and through whom we ourselves exist became flesh and dwelt among us (John 1.14). He reflects the glory of God and bears the very stamp of his nature, upholding the universe by his word of power (Hebrews 1.3). The Incarnation makes him both the image of the invisible God and the first-born of all creation. It was in him that all things were created, in heaven and on earth, visible and invisible. In him all things hold together (Colossians 1.15–17). The Incarnate Lord is therefore not only the Word and Wisdom of God in creation, but also the model and the fulfilment (in the Greek, the *pleroma*) of all things. The ultimate purpose of history is the reconciliation of God and the world (2 Corinthians 5.17–19; Colossians 1.10), the bringing of everything under him as under one head (Ephesians 1.20). The whole span of history from Creation to the Last Day is totally "in Christ", a movement in time of the entire cosmos from the "first" to the "last" creation (Ephesians 2.15; 4.25; Romans 8.19–24a). The Word through whom all things were made is therefore not only the Word of Creation and the Word of Revelation of God's ultimate purpose; he is also the Word of Redemption and the Word of Consummation (Ephesians 1.7–9): the secret of history is the "secret of Christ" (Colossians 2.2).

Through the preaching of Jesus Christ, this mystery – which was kept secret for long ages – is now disclosed. Through the prophetic writings it is made known to all nations, according to the command of the eternal God. Until the blowing of the seventh trumpet on the Last Day (Revelation 10.7), the revelation of this mystery is intended to bring about the obedience of faith (Romans 16.25–27).

If it is not easy to say what the Christian understanding of time should be, even the most cursory examination of the Bible should suffice to prove that Christians are expected to experience time "in Christ". Christ's love leaves us no choice: we must not only believe that history follows a law of purpose and design, but also offer ourselves with the crucified Lord – a single, holy and living sacrifice – as instruments (in the Latin, *ministri*) of the coming of God's kingdom. Of our three original questions, only the last one remains still unanswered: should the specifically Christian experience of time be made to lie at the heart of the structure of our liturgical calendars and lectionaries?

This question can be answered at two different levels. We may feel tempted to regard liturgical calendars and lectionaries as mere educational tools destined to relieve the general ignorance of most Christian people. For many a modern lectionary the temptation has proved too great and some educationalists would gladly take us even further along this doubtful road. An answer at this level will simply not do. The liturgy of the Church must be *kerygma* before it becomes *didache*. In this view, the whole of the liturgy would be at best the repository of useful material for the intellectual and moral advancement of the individual Christian. Thanks to Louis Bouyer and many other liturgical scholars we now know that the liturgy of the Church is nothing less than the realisation of the very Mystery of Christ which, as we have seen, lies at the core of the Christian message and of the Christian experience of time".

For Louis Bouyer, the Mystery of Christ is both an historical fact and an historical process. It is an historical *fact* in that it has been accomplished once and for all and can never be begun again. But the irrepeatable event of the death of our Saviour has brought into existence a reality which is to fill all time: a *process* which is intended to make God all in all and everything to everyone (1 Corinthians 15–28). Christ is now the Second Adam, the heavenly Man, the ultimate Man, in whom all human beings are to die in order to live again in Christ's own divine life.

The process involved in the Mystery of Christ is a very wide and comprehensive one. No one phase of it could have value by itself or be partaken of by itself: to partake of the Mystery is to partake of Christ, who will re-enact in us everything which has been achieved in himself, through his own action once and for all. Within the unity of Christ's Mystery, even the Cross and Resurrection can be distinguished only as that to which everything tended which happened before, and from which everything proceeds which is to happen hereafter.

The wholeness of the Mystery of Christ does not imply any lack of a well-defined structure. On the contrary, within this complex process we can distinguish *two* processes, the *first* of which in some ways not only produces, but includes the other. The first of these two processes is the "passage" ("Passover") of Christ from death to life. The second is our own "passage" ("Passover"), that is the "passage" or "Passover" of the Church. The second "Passover" is fully precontained in the first. The goal of the second "Passover" is that we should reach the goal of the first and "attain ... the perfect Man (in the Greek, *eis andra teleion*), to the mature fulness of the stature of Christ" (Ephesians 4.13). On the one hand, the process reproduces that of the historical life of our Lord. On the other hand, there is indeed here and now a process of death and resurrection which we must make our own.

We enter this process at three different levels: at our own baptism, at every celebration of the Eucharist, and in the sequence of the Mystery's historical process as set forth in the liturgical year. For Bouyer, the necessity of these three different ways of meeting the Mystery of Christ is clearly the consequence of the nature of time. Just as our natural life also grows by means of large cycles made up of many days, so does our Christian life. The liturgy takes the natural year, the cycle of human life which is in harmony with the rhythms of the cosmos, and presents the great phases of the Mystery which we are to undergo throughout the year's recurring days, so that when we come to die, we shall have been made ready for death, not only by the natural rhythm of created and fallen human life, but also by the supernatural rhythms of supernatural life, as these are grafted on our natural living.

The Mystery of Christ is what the Church proclaims. In the Church here and now, as in the beginning of the world, God speaks and his Word is accomplished. The meaning and reality of the liturgical year depend on these truths. Seen as a whole, the liturgical year is the great and permanent proclamation (*kerygma*) by the Church of the Word with which she has been entrusted. When the liturgy is all set out within the framework of the liturgical year, this framework contains not only an *expression* of the Mystery of Christ, but also the *reality* of that Mystery, working by faith through love and tending towards its final realisation. For the Word of the Mystery cannot be so solemnly proclaimed by the Church, in, with and through the risen Lord, without creating thereby what it proclaims.

No liturgical calendar and lectionary, ancient or modern, makes sense apart from the Church's proclamation of the Mystery of Christ. As Bouyer realised only too well, the problem is not whether the Mystery of Christ should lie at the heart of the structure of liturgical calendars and lectionaries but:

> The real problem arises with the further question: how are we to understand in more detail the appropriation of different elements and phases of the Mystery to the different festivals and seasons of the liturgical year? Does the development of the Mystery adapt itself somehow to the development of the liturgical year? And if so, how, then, are we to understand its adaptation?[2]

The unfolding of the Christian year was an organic, unplanned development from Jewish roots. At a certain point in the history of the Church, that development was arrested. As a result, we have the problem of the sporadic existence of "liturgical seasons" within an otherwise season-less yearly cycle. The problem is of course particularly acute in the period after Pentecost. Moreover, we have a certain lack of definition in one of the liturgical seasons; the season of Advent. As Bouyer demonstrates, the ancient liturgical texts of the Western Church for the season of Advent express not the expectation of a Nativity which has already happened, but the expectation of the Parousia which is still to come: "we find there not the hope of what is now called the first coming of Christ (for how can we still hope for it?), but the hope of his final coming on the clouds of heaven".[3] Nevertheless, the Advent period has been traditionally structured into four separate and unco-ordinated weeks. The choice of readings in most lectionaries is both confusing and confused. All we can find is the hopeless and recurrent intertwining of the two themes of final judgement and expectation of the Messiah, instead of what we should most certainly be entitled to find: the *one* theme of the inevitable consummation of God's eschatological plan as already pre-determined and contained in the mystery of the Incarnation.

Most liturgical calendars have been extremely cautious on this point and have chosen to err, if necessary, on the side of tradition. One wonders if we should not follow the example of some Oriental Christian Churches and introduce further liturgical seasons after Pentecost. One also wonders if we should not be adventurous enough to try and find ways of getting rid of the "per annum" ("throughout the year") concept altogether, as the Joint Liturgical Group of Great Britain has already done in a limited way.

To give but one example, the liturgical year of the East-Syrian Church is organised around the date of Easter and, in a secondary way, around the festivals of Christmas and the Epiphany. The whole liturgical year is divided into nine liturgical seasons, the last of which is the season of the Dedication of the Church to God's purpose.[4] Could we not do the same and perhaps even improve on the original idea? We could divide the liturgical year into two sub-cycles. The first uninterrupted group of seasons, from the beginning of the year to the end of the season of Pentecost, would re-propose "the Mystery of Christ for his Church". These seasons would represent the God-manward movement of the announcement of the coming Kingdom and of the enablement of the People of God to be instruments of that coming. The second uninterrupted sub-cycle of seasons, from after Pentecost to the end of the year, would re-propose "the Mystery of the Church for Christ" and re-present the secondary, derivative, but equally essential man-Godward movement of the Church's enabled response to God's grace. A liturgical season of the Dedication of the Church to God's Purpose, followed by a season of Advent in the sense advocated by Bouyer, would be seen much more clearly as the breaking point of the yearly cycle (*"anni circulus"*) into an ever ascending *spiral* of continuous growth brought about by the future consummation of all things in Christ. In this sense, the succession of liturgical year after liturgical year would clearly refer to the overall "process" involved in the totality of the Mystery of Christ.

Any decision about the liturgical calendar is bound to influence a decision about the liturgical lectionary. Seasonal themes and continuous or semi-continuous reading of the Bible are not easily reconciled. Almost universally, the principle of *"lectio semi-continua"* breaks down during liturgical seasons. The most that can be expected is proper readings for the major festivals and semi-continuous reading of certain books of the Bible for the main body of the liturgical seasons. This latter practice is not without its merits, as it combines the best of both worlds.

The Roman Lectionary and the Common Lectionary of North America recognise this difficulty and prescribe proper readings for festivals and seasons together with semi-continuous reading for the *"tempus per annum"*. But why introduce what might well appear as the anomaly of "ordinary time"? And are not the Epistles, the book of Acts and the book of Revelation worthy to be read and expanded on their own merit? Why only the Synoptic Gospels and some parts of the Old Testament? Why the special and very much secondary treatment of the Gospel of John? One cannot help suspecting here a certain lack of vision and planning.

The Church has survived nearly two millennia without a fully articulated and ecumenically-agreed plan for its liturgical calendar and lectionary. It would be foolish therefore to pretend that, unless the best possible articulated plan was found, the proclamation of the Church would cease to be the authentic proclamation of the Mystery of Christ. But it would be equally foolish to pretend that, *without* such a plan, the Church's proclamation would be just as effective.

During the many centuries of the Church's existence, the clear vision of the meaning of time enshrined in ancient liturgical documents such as the Sacramentary of Verona has become progressively obscured through the influence of successive cultures and events. Today the passing of time itself and specific historical events are not often seen in the light of God's mysterious and ultimate purpose for creation. Post-Christendom Man has largely lost this specifically Christian vision, and with it its hope. Many of our contemporaries, believers and unbelievers alike, are unconcerned with the past and hold little hope for the future. For many, only the present counts. For some, time has no meaning except that of a commodity which may be bought or sold for the greater enjoyment of the present.[5] Following in this the late-medieval "fuga mundi" theory of spirituality, many devout Christians today seek meaning in a flight from the supposedly "profane" to the supposedly "sacred". Their vision of time and their understanding of the purpose and function of the liturgy of the Church are therefore very largely not Christian but pagan.

It is this kind of society we address when we propose liturgical calendars and lectionaries. How clear must we therefore be in proposing the Word of Christ's Mystery to those who are bidden to tread the path of Christ's sufferings in growing conformity to his death, to know the power of his resurrection, and to make up in their own bodies for what is still lacking in the passion of the risen Lord (Philemon 3.10; Colossians 1.24)? Formulated in this way, the question answers itself.

NOTES

1 L. Bouyer, *Life and Liturgy*, 1954, pp. 185–228.
2 L. Bouyer, op. cit., p. 189.
3 ibid., p. 203.
4 J. Mateos, *Essai d'Intérpretation des Matines Chaldéennes*, Lelya-Sapra, Rome 1959, pp. 14–15.
5 C. H. B. Meyer, *Time and Liturgy: Anthropological Notes on the Nature of Time* in W. Vos and G. Wainwright (eds.) *Liturgical Time*, Rotterdam, 1982, pp. 4–22.

8

IS A CALENDAR NEEDED?

✠

Maurice Williams

As human beings we are creatures of time, and we measure its passing. We count the hours of our days, the days of our years and years of our history. We count them as recurring units of time, from which we have devised systems fixing the beginning and length of years, and then within the years we have marked convenient sub-divisions. Calendars are an inevitable fact of human life.

The nature of a year in the course of one cycle of its seasons is a fundamental unit of measured time. It is used to define the age of a person or the reign of a king. It is used to prepare for those activities which depend on its seasons, such as sowing and reaping. It is then used to plan the annual repetition of activities which are not to a climatic season, for example, a school's Speech Day or the Promenade Concerts. In consequence, it has influenced the practice of most religions, especially those whose festivals are related primarily to the pattern of agriculture.

In framing a Liturgical Year, the Church is accepting that measured unit, so that Christmas and Easter, like birthdays or the Boat Race, come round once a year. The Christian festivals, however, are not simply recurring. They recall events which have happened once for all in the past, declaring those events to be the good news of our salvation for all time.

When the Church was born, it inherited two other time units within the system of counting by years. One of these was the lunar month. The Jewish Passover, for instance, was kept each year, but not on a fixed date. It was a moveable feast, according to the phases of the moon. The Christian Easter, originally coinciding with it, has continued to be dated by the same calculation.

The other sub-divisional unit was the seven-day week. This also was received from the Jews, who lived in a succession of weeks, each of which ended with a sabbath day.

Our culture is familiar with months of the year, although mainly by named units of variable length which have been imposed on the annual calendar. It is also familiar with the seven-day week. We should therefore bear in mind that in the ancient world lunar months were common, but that the week was peculiarly Jewish. There is good reason to think this Jewish time-scale was influential in the Roman Empire of the first century A.D. Our present names for the days of the week derive from astrology, but the probability is that such a "planetary" week developed in association with the Jewish week.

The focus of the Jewish week was its final sabbath day. The other days were of little importance except that they led up to this one, so that they were known simply as first, second, third, and so on. The Church inherited this pattern. It followed the practice of demarcating one day as the significant point of the week, but it altered the day from the seventh to the first.

With the probable exception of an annual Easter which remained associated with the Jewish feast of Passover, the earliest Christian calendar was framed by a weekly Lord's Day, for so the first day of the week came to be called. Both the choice of the day and the name for it are emphatic. On the one hand, it was a break from the sabbath, thereby carrying overtones of our Lord's Messianic breaking of the sabbath rules during the days of his flesh. On the other hand, it was explicitly related to the risen Christ, proclaiming the day on which he was raised and declaring that on this day of worship the exalted Lord was present with and known to his People.

It seems likely that with the abandoning of the sabbath, Christians were encouraged to keep *every* day holy. Nonetheless, the Lord's Day governed the week. (This name, indeed, is preserved in the romance languages and in several Eastern countries, although it has been displaced by "Sunday" of the planetary week in the Germanic and Anglo-Saxon tongues).

It should be noted that because the Lord's Day was the first day of the week there emerged a Christian awareness that its worship also celebrated God's creative work. Moreover, its symbolic name as "the eighth day" appeared as well. This represented the belief that in Christ's dying and rising God's new creation had been inaugurated. Although this later dropped out of use, perhaps because it was obscure, its eschatalogical perspective was retained. The Advent hope informed the liturgy through and through. So every Lord's Day was an Easter Day. It was also a Christmas Day, a Pentecost and an Advent Day. It was the primary festival of the fulness of the Gospel.

The Gospel's centre of gravity, however, is the dying and rising of Jesus Christ. That event was historically linked to the Jewish Passover. It is likely, as has been mentioned above, that an annual Easter was observed in the Church from the beginning. In this manner the unit of the year was superimposed on the weekly feast of the Lord's Day but, as the Passover occurred on the day of a full moon, which might happen on any day of the week, some Christians wished to keep Easter on the day of the Passover whenever it was, whereas others were convinced it should be kept on the Lord's Day. The latter group eventually got their way, with Easter being dated on the first Sunday after the Passover full moon. This was the first calendrical dispute, now known as the Quartodeciman controversy.

Thus Easter gave impetus to the development of the Christian Year, for Pentecost coincided with the Jewish Feast of Weeks, fifty days after Passover. By Christian computation, that kept Pentecost on a Sunday too.

Thereafter, the story is a familiar one. An annual Pentecost provided a fixed period after Easter, suggesting the use of the intervening time between the two as an Easter season and allowing for the dating of Ascension Day in due course on the fortieth day after Easter. Then, as Easter day in the West became the customary day for initiation into the membership of the Church, the weeks prior to it gradually

assumed the character of serious preparation for discipleship. Only after some centuries was there a need felt to
mark the birth of our Lord in a similar way. In the East,
January 6th was chosen for this, whereas in the West
December 25th became the appointed date. (Significantly,
perhaps, there was no pressure to tie Christmas Day, or
Ascension Day, to a Sunday). Thereafter, Christmas also
gained its preparatory period, known as Advent, but this
showed considerable variation both in length and content
from place to place. Likewise, a Christmas or Epiphany
season evolved in the weeks following the feast of the
Nativity.

The span of time from Advent to Pentecost is approxi-
mately six months, half a year, the unit of the year being
what it is in human life. So far so good. There is everything
to gain from such a calendar which rehearses the events of
the Gospel. But then comes an awkward hiatus, the other
half of the year has to be lived through before we can start
again. This was eventually bridged with a succession of
"Sundays after Pentecost".

The first half-year was not entirely without its problems
either. When the pre-Easter period of preparation was
settled as six weeks, the Christmas or Epiphany season had
a variable length according to the date of Easter. Or again,
there was not a universal length for Advent. The more Sundays it traversed, the fewer there were needed after Pentecost. The medieval Church in the West managed its own
reduction of one of the latter by instituting a festival in
honour of the Holy Trinity on the first after Pentecost and
then tabling "Sundays after Trinity".

Throughout the period of this development of an annual
progressing of feasts, another Christian use of the time unit
of a year was being concurrently expanded. Particular days
were set aside for the commemoration of particular saints.
These, as Holy Days, increased in number with the passing
of the centuries. The two forms of Calendar served quite
different purposes. When they were mingled, confusion
must have reigned in the minds of many Christian people.

After the upheaval of the Reformation, the Protestant
Churches almost entirely removed the calendar of Holy

Days. Some of them also chose to ignore the calendar of the Liturgical Year, even to the extent of not observing Christmas and Easter. What was influencing them, consciously or unconsciously, was the problem of conflating the unit of the week, represented by the joy of the Lord's Day, with the unit of the year.

At this point the strong connection between observing the Calendar and following a Lectionary should be noted. In the centuries since the Reformation, those Churches which retained the yearly Calendar have shown substantial agreement in their arrangement of it, although there are some variations of date and emphasis. The Anglicans and Lutherans, for example, stayed with Trinity Sunday, whereas the Roman Catholics kept to Sundays after Pentecost. All of them followed a lectionary, but each devised its own.

The Churches which rejected the Calendar at first have gradually restored some of its focal points. Only in very recent years, however, have they adopted the use of a lectionary, and then mainly as the choice of some ministers in some congregations. Such Churches, in Britain at least, now meet for worship on Christmas Day. An increasing number of them have a late night service on Christmas Eve as well. Similarly they gather on Good Friday, and perhaps on Maundy Thursday also. Most of them have added Palm Sunday to their calendar, and all of them keep Pentecost. In some of them, Lent and Advent are observed, and in a very few of them Ascension Day.

With a skeletal calendar like this, a lectionary is not usually followed, and yet on the marked days lections are chosen with a "seasonal" content; but once even a very few days are so marked, the unit of the year has re-appeared. What then is done with the overwhelming majority of Sundays which are unmarked? They are plundered frequently on behalf of some special cause, be it national or local. Choir Sunday, Education Sunday, Church Anniversary and the like fill in the gaps. Furthermore, *the* High Day of the year, at least for many of the worshippers, is Harvest Thanksgiving.

The majority of the Churches in Britain, whether they follow the Liturgical Year or not, find room for Bible Sunday, the Octave for Unity, Christian Aid Week and Remembrance Day.

The Joint Liturgical Group published its reconsideration of the Calendar and Lectionary in 1967. After listening to the whole Tradition, it endorsed the liturgical practice of the Christian Year, with its three foci of Christmas, Easter and Pentecost, as the means by which the worshipping Church lives over again the saving deeds of the Lord.

Accepting the Year's fundamental structure, and noting that the Tradition shows some variations in detail, the Group proposed some modest reforms of its own. As an attempt to clarify the objectives of the Calendar, it removed Epiphany – the old Eastern date for the feast of our Lord's incarnation – and suggested several Sundays "after Christmas" to run through to the beginning of the Easter cycle. Here it provided nine Sundays "before Easter", retaining the Lenten title for the last six of them but removing the names of Septuagesima, Sexagesima and Quinquagesima from the first three. With an eye on the Lectionary which marches with the Calendar, it argued that this sequence allowed space to move through the major events in the life of Jesus and on to his Passion without interruption. Next, and also with an eye on an improved Lectionary, it proposed a similar period of nine Sundays "before Christmas", allowing the last four to be marked "in Advent". This made room for the Old Testament to be prominent as the background of the Gospel. Finally, it proposed a return to the nomenclature of Sundays "after Pentecost", on the ground that Trinity Sunday was the commemoration not so much of an event as of a doctrine. The accompanying Lectionary for this succession of Sundays, over almost half a year, allows us to move on from Pentecost, as the Church sent out into the world to live the Spirit-filled life.

This Calendar has received substantial approval from the Churches in Britain, although it has been amended in a few particulars by those who have adopted it. It has, however, met with two criticisms. On the one hand, some people responsible for preparing a syllabus of Christian education in the Free Churches found it to be unduly restrictive for their purpose. In this they were justified. Their criticism was directed mainly at the accompanying Lectionary, but the only response that could be made to them was an affirmation that the keeping of the Christian Year is not primarily a teaching aid. It is a celebration of the Gospel.

The other criticism, peculiarly enough, came from the opposite direction. The Standing Committee of the American Episcopal Church judged that the inherent fallacy of such an approach to the Christian year lay in its basis, which it deemed to be pedagogical rather than kerygmatic. Peter Cobb[1] endorsed this judgement. He considered that the Joint Liturgical Group's proposals depart radically from the traditions of the early Church and show little appreciation of the theological meaning of the Christian Year as a means of participating in the mystery of Christ. "Pentecost is given a new prominence by becoming a third focus of the Christian Year. ... The controlling factor in adjusting the length of the seasons has been less their intrinsic nature and purpose than considerations of lectional convenience. The pre-Christmas season, for example, has been lengthened in order to allow for readings covering salvation-history from creation to the Nativity". Perhaps the only response to this, apart from noting how the pedagogues themselves reacted, is to confess that Calendar and Lectionary do belong together, and to reaffirm that the intention behind their shape and structure *is* kerygmatic.

Finally, two contemporary questions about the making of a Christian Calendar require notice. The first, raised explicitly by W. Rordorf[2] as long ago as 1962, asks how much longer we can assume the primary unit of the week as a working basis. The industrialising of the Western economy has led to a demand for a re-examination of the traditional pattern of work and leisure. The working week is now reckoned in hours rather than days. In the foreseeable future, Rordorf remarks, the protection by law of the day of rest and worship after every six days may no longer apply. He therefore argues that Sunday as a day of rest came to be the custom *after* it had been established as the day of worship, so that whatever happens in society about the day(s) of rest, "Sunday as the day for worship is nothing less than one of the central elements in the Christian life".

The second question looks at the unit of the year in a similar fashion. Until recent years, Pentecost had become a secular holiday as well as a Christian festival. Then the secular holiday was given a fixed date, while Pentecost remained moveable in relation to Easter and more often than not did not coincide with the secular holiday. A desire in the Church itself to have Easter as a fixed date has gathered increasing strength. (The Joint Liturgical Group's Calendar allows for this possibility, with Easter Day occurring between April 9th and 16th). Such a decision does not look likely in the immediate future, but if it were to come, the Church's Year would not only be cut loose from lunar calculations but also coincide again with secular holidays. Experience suggests that the three major festivals of the Church, round which the Calendar is constructed, are affected in different ways by the secular calendar of work. Easter, as the Gospel's centre of gravity, remains what it is, whatever its date. Pentecost seems to have benefited in the years when its Sunday was not part of a national Bank Holiday. Christmas has been under pressure for some time now, with carol services galore being arranged by popular demand weeks ahead of their proper time.

NOTES

1 *The Study of Liturgy*, edited by Jones, Wainwright and Yarnold (1978) pp. 418–419. The document of the American Episcopal Church's Standing Liturgical Commission which Cobb approves is available in *Prayer Book Studies 19* (Church Hymnal Corporation, New York).
2 *Sunday* by Willy Rordorf (1962) p. 1.

9

THE ROMAN CALENDAR

✠

Edward Matthews

The newspaper called it a "shock". Jewellers and souvenir manufacturers trembled with fear. Experts were interviewed on TV about the possible repercussions upon Western Christianity. The cause of such excitement? The abolition of St. Christopher.

Abolition is a strong word. What had happened was that on 9th May 1969 a wholesale reform of the Roman Calendar was launched upon the world, and Christopher, a saint whose origins are lost in the myths of time, was seen to have been removed from the universal calendar. He was not the only saint to suffer the same fate, nor was this the most important part of the reform, but it certainly caught the journalistic imagination. There is no evidence, however, that the sales of travellers' medallions declined appreciably.

The new Roman Calendar had received the approval of Pope Paul VI on 14th February 1969, but was by no means the only such reform in recent times. Pius XII had introduced changes in 1955, and in the same year had carried out a long-awaited reform of Holy Week. John XXIII put his name to an extensive list of Calendar changes in 1960, but the more fundamental re-examination was left to the initiative of the Second Vatican Council.

The Constitution on the Sacred Liturgy (4th December 1963), paragraph 107, states:

> The Liturgical year is to be revised so that the traditional customs and discipline of the sacred seasons shall be preserved or restored to suit the conditions of modern times.

Their specific character is to be retained so that they
duly nourish the piety of the faithful who celebrate the
mysteries of the Christian redemption and, above all, the
paschal mystery . . .

This directive is part of the short but pithy Chapter V which
deals with the meaning of the liturgical year and therefore
constitutes the foundation upon which the subsequent reform was to be built.

The Roman Calendar is a legal document; the reality it
regulates is of a far higher order, the mystery of Christ. By
this is to be understood the making present in liturgical
celebration of all the major stages of the work of our redemption, incarnation, birth, ministry, passion, resurrection, ascension and coming of the Spirit, as well as
anticipation of his second coming.[1] All these events are
celebrated liturgically on a regular cycle in such a way that,
by participation in the celebration, the Christian partici-
pates in the redemption event itself.

Consequently the liturgical cycle, as understood by the
Roman Calendar, should not be seen as a simply moral
participation in Christ's saving acts, or as a succession of
marvels presented for our admiration and example. On
the contrary, the cycle is the re-presentation of the
Paschal Mystery itself, so that by our celebration of the
events we may become one with them in a sacramental but
real sense.

Easter, therefore, stands at the centre of the liturgical
year rather as Sunday stands to the rest of the days of the
week (CR 18). The whole of Christ's earthly life may be
regarded as a "passing over" to the Father, and in that
sense the entire liturgical year celebrates his Paschal Mystery. But the climax of Christ's "passing over" took place in
his actual dying and rising. For that reason the celebration
of Easter is seen by the Roman Calendar as commencing on
Maundy Thursday evening with the Evening Mass of the
Lord's Supper, and continuing through to its climax in the
Easter Vigil Service. The three days of the Easter Triduum,
with the services which mark each day, are to be looked
upon as one festal celebration.

The Roman Calendar receives its fulfilment in the Lectionary, Missal and Rite for the Christian Initiation of Adults. These provide the resources for the celebration of Easter and situate the three sacraments of Christian Initiation, Baptism, Confirmation and Eucharist, in the rightful setting – the Easter Vigil. The new life attained by the dead and risen Christ is entered into by candidates anxious to be counted part of his mystical body.

The celebration of Easter does not end on Easter Sunday. It continues for seven weeks and ends on the fiftieth day, Pentecost Sunday (CR 22). That this period should be regarded as one complete celebration of the Easter mystery is quite intentional. The Roman Calendar names the weeks following Easter Sunday as "the weeks of Easter", whereas the pre-1969 calendar named them "after Easter".

The change from "after" to "of" is important. It indicates that in the mind of the Church there is an essential link between the dying, rising, ascending of Jesus and the coming of the Spirit. They are one movement in the economy of redemption. For the same reason Pentecost no longer sports an octave: it comes as the conclusion of the Paschal Mystery rather than as the commencement of a new period of celebration.

The time before Easter, Lent, is a time of preparation (CR 27), preparation for baptism by catechumens, and for the renewal of baptism by those already members of the community. The Roman Calendar is "fleshed out" by the Lectionary, which contains a three-year cycle of readings for the Sundays of Lent, the first cycle being especially selected for baptismal preparation. The Rite for the Christian Initiation of Adults provides additional ritual material for the same purpose. In this way the Roman Calendar of 1969 makes far clearer than its predecessor what is the length, and meaning, of Lent. The Sundays of Septuagesima, Sexagesima and Quinquagesima have been abolished.

It is noteworthy that the reform of the Roman Calendar, and its attendant liturgical texts, is bringing about a perceptible change in attitude on the part of Western Roman Catholics. Easter is being increasingly regarded at a popular level as of greater importance than Christmas, this despite commercial pressures to the contrary.

Nevertheless Christmas has its own importance (CR 32). As a season it extends to the feast of the Baptism of the Lord, celebrated on the Sunday following Epiphany. In this way the entire season is concerned with the manifestation of the Lord.

Such, too, with a sense of joyful expectancy, is the concern of Advent (CR 39). It begins on the Sunday nearest 30 November, and acts as a period of preparation for the Nativity and the Second Coming of Christ at the end of time.

A major aim of the present Roman Calendar is the restoration of the Sunday as a liturgical day in its own right. Before the recent liturgical reforms it was a sad fact that saints' days of little importance displaced the normal Sunday celebration. Now that has changed dramatically, a change initiated by Vatican II:

> By a tradition handed down by the apostles, which took its origin from the very day of Christ's resurrection, the Church celebrates the paschal mystery every eighth day, which day is appropriately called the Lord's Day or Sunday. ... The Lord's Day is the original feast day. ... Other celebrations, unless they be truly of the greatest importance, shall not have precedence over Sunday, which is the foundation and kernel of the whole liturgical year. (*Constitution on the Sacred Liturgy*, para. 106).

These principles have been given legal force by the Roman Calendar (CR 4). It is now very difficult indeed to displace a Sunday by another celebration. The celebrations of the Holy Family, the Baptism of the Lord, the Trinity, and Christ the King are permanently assigned to Sundays, and celebrations such as Saints Peter and Paul, the Assumption, and All Saints may occasionally occur on a Sunday and displace it, but apart from those the Sunday has been restored intact by the Calendar.

Sadly, local initiative sometimes overcomes the desires of Vatican II. National episcopal conferences may, and frequently do, designate certain Sundays as days of prayer for particular causes. Laudable in itself perhaps, but this is frequently translated as an excuse to replace the Sunday celebration with another, often with the theme of social justice.

The Sundays which occur outside Advent, Christmastide, Lent and Eastertide are weighed down by the title, "Sundays of the Year", or, "Ordinary Sundays of the Year". A not altogether happy title, it replaces the former season known as "Sundays after Pentecost". A change in title was necessary because "Sundays of the Year" include not only those which occur between Pentecost and Advent, but also between the end of Christmastide (the Baptism of the Lord) and Lent. There are 34 altogether, but, because of the movement of Easter, one of these is frequently, though not always, omitted.

Finally, the importance of the Sunday has been considerably enhanced by the provision of a three-year cycle of Readings and a revised, enlarged collection of prayer texts.

Saints

Little of the basic reforms of the Roman Calendar, described above, found room in the newspapers. It was left to the saints to enjoy the limelight. Paradoxically they did so because, officially at least, they were about to leave it. Undoubtedly reform of the celebrations of Saints' Days was an urgent need, and since 1969 there has been little regret at the extent of the reform.

Witnesses to the faith have been accorded a privileged place in the Church's memory from early times. "For the feasts of Saints proclaim the wonderful works of Christ in his servants and offer to the faithful fitting examples for their imitation".[2]

The veneration of saints is best seen in the light of the Paschal Mystery. Christian communities, at various times and in various places, have recognised in certain of their brethren a closer conformity to the image of Christ than is usual. They are seen manifestly to be patterning their lives on his. On occasions this has led to the ultimate sacrifice of martyrdom. At the same time, their life of witness has provided an example of Christian living and therefore evidence of the accomplishment of God's will in man and womankind. The celebration of a saint is really praise of God for his work in us. But like all good things, this could be taken too far. Pope Pius V in his reform of the Divine Office (1568) and of the Missal (1570) sanctioned a calendar which included 158 saints' celebrations. Just before Vatican II the number had grown to 338. The Roman Calendar of 1969 cut back the number of such possible celebrations to 191, 95 of which can be ignored (and are) if local communities so wish.

It was not only that there were too many saints. A problem arose, indicated earlier, at the ease with which saints' celebrations (Proper of the Saints) frequently displaced more important seasonal celebrations (Proper of the Time). Furthermore, many of these saints were of little interest outside their own home territory, and not a few appeared to owe their existence more to legend than to reality.

Also included under the general title, Proper of the Saints, was a collection of "feasts of devotion", mostly celebrations of the Virgin Mary, though not exclusively so. These owed their existence to particular events (e.g. Our Lady of the Rosary to commemorate the anniversary of the victory of the Christian naval forces over the Turks at Lepanto), because of the devotion of particular religious orders, or pious associations. Many had outlived their usefulness. The majority of these celebrations have been left to the choice of local communities and thus removed from the universal calendar. Reforming the list of saints was not easy, and we will not enter into detail here. The principle criteria for inclusion in the Calendar were:

(a) Historicity. A weeding out of Saints of dubious origin.
(b) The reduction of the number of saints from Roman antiquity. It should be noted that the Calendar of Pius V was made up largely of holy men and women from the city of Rome.
(c) The reduction of the number of Popes from thirty eight to fifteen.

(d) The selection of saints with more universal appeal, and the elimination of others. Therefore, added to the list are saints from Japan, Canada, U.S.A. and Africa.

Local Calendars

The Roman Calendar is, despite its name, a universal calendar. For that reason many Italian and Roman (city) saints were removed from the list of universal celebrations. The same can be said, in a proportionate manner, of saints of other countries. Therefore the Roman Calendar encourages and directs the drawing up of local calendars for the use of dioceses, nations, or religious orders. (CR 49). In this way smaller groups, or communities, are enabled to celebrate saints who have a special connection with them.[3] Generally speaking these calendars are short and add little to the universal version. For example, the diocese of Westminster has an additional 15 celebrations, in which figure such saints as St. Alban, St. Laurence, St. David.

Grades of Celebration

Celebrations of persons or events are graded as follows:

> Solemnity
> Feast
> Memorial
> Optional memorial.

In this way is the balance of the Calendar protected. A Solemnity may not be replaced by a Feast if the two happen to occur on the same day (e.g. if the Feast of St. Matthew should clash with the First Sunday of Lent, which counts as a Solemnity). The same applies in descending order to the grades of Memorial and Optional Memorial.

Weekdays with no particular celebration assigned to them are termed "Feria". Despite the lack of particular celebration, every day of the year has its own Readings taken from the Lectionary cycle. Ferias of the major seasons of the year (Advent, Lent, etc.) take precedence over Memorials. The "flavour" of the season is thus retained.

Even during ordinary times of the year Memorials are quite frequently marked at Mass merely by the recitation of a special opening prayer. The rest – Readings and prayers – is taken from the Feria. The same applies to the texts of the Divine Office on such a day.

Optional Memorials are what their title suggests: a celebrant is at liberty to choose or omit that particular saint assigned to that class. As we noted earlier, there are 95 optional Memorials, and it is probably true to say that the majority are omitted by most celebrants.

Conclusion

The 1969 Roman Calendar brought relief and reason to the Church's liturgy. All saints and celebrations are in some way related to Christ. However the passage of time had ensured that wood could not be seen for the trees. The new Calendar cleared away that which was unnecessary and unbalanced.

However this clearing away was itself the fruit of a renewed understanding of the nature of the liturgical year, the ever recurring participation, through celebration, in the mystery of our redemption.

NOTES

1 Father, may we celebrate the eucharist with reverence and love, for when we proclaim the death of the Lord you continue the work of his redemption, who is Lord for ever and ever. *Calendarium Romanum* (CR), para. 17.

2 *Constitution on the Sacred Liturgy*, para III.

3 See also *Constitution on the Sacred Liturgy*, para III.

10

THE RECONCILIATION OF CALENDARS

A. Raymond George

Two lectionaries are in widespread use: the two-year cycle in *The Calendar and Lectionary* of the Joint Liturgical Group (JLG) and the three-year cycle, either in the form of the current Roman Catholic lectionary or in the modification of the Roman scheme known as *The Common Lectionary* (CL), prepared by the Consultation on Common Texts. The question naturally arises whether the best features of these could somehow be combined. A preliminary difficulty is that they use different calendars; each of them has produced its own variation from the traditional Western arrangement of the Christian year. This table shows the contrast, though in the nature of the case it can show it only roughly, for the difficulty is that the two schemes differ in more than the names of the Sundays.

Joint Liturgical Group	*Common Lectionary*
9th to 5th before Christmas	(end of previous year)
4th to 1st before Christmas	1st to 4th of/in Advent
(= Advent 1–4)	
Christmas Day	Christmas Day
Christmas 1–6	Christmas 1
	January 1st
	Christmas 2
	Epiphany
	Baptism (Epiphany 1)
	Epiphany 2–5
9th to 7th before Easter	Epiphany 6–8 (Propers 1–3)
	Last after Epiphany
	(Transfiguration)

Joint Liturgical Group	*Common Lectionary*
Ash Wednesday	Ash Wednesday
6th to 1st before Easter	1st to 5th of/in Lent
(= Lent 1–4, Passion, Palm)	Passion/Palm
	Holy Week
Good Friday	Easter Vigil
Easter Day	Easter
Easter 1–5	2nd to 6th of Easter
Ascension Day	Ascension
Easter 6	7th of Easter
Pentecost	Pentecost
Pentecost 1 (Trinity)–21	Trinity
(Beginning of following year)	Propers 9–29 (Christ the King)

JLG also provides for the Epiphany, when it is observed on January 6th, and in its more recent book *Holy Week Services* provides for Holy Week and the Easter Vigil, and CL has certain special days such as All Saints.

Some of the discrepancies relate simply to the name of the day. Thus CL treats Easter Day as the 1st Sunday of Easter, and thus what JLG calls Easter 1 is in CL the 2nd Sunday of Easter, and so on. There are, however, discrepancies which make it impossible to say that such and such a Sunday in JLG is simply another name for such and such a Sunday in CL or vice versa. Is there any possibility of reconciling at least the calendars? Even if it proved difficult to reconcile the lectionaries, an agreed calendar might well be worthwhile for its own sake.

It is first necessary to consider the major changes which the Roman Lectionary and CL have introduced. The Roman Lectionary, as someone has remarked, has simplified things in a complicated way. The old tradition, as exemplified, in the *Book of Common Prayer* 1662, was that the Sundays after Epiphany ran on till they gave place to "The Sunday called Septuagesima, or the third Sunday before Lent", which was in fact the ninth Sunday before Easter, and began what might be called pre-Lent. There could be any number of Sundays from one to six after Epiphany according to the date of Easter. Similarly the Sundays after Trinity ran on till they gave place to the first Sunday in Advent. Some churches not in the Anglican tradition, notably the Roman, reckoned them after Pentecost,

83

adding of course one to the numbers. The Sundays after Trinity could vary in number from twenty-two to twenty-seven, but provision was made for only twenty-five, and after that came this rubric "If there be any more Sundays before Advent Sunday, the Service of some of those Sundays that were omitted after the Epiphany shall be taken in to supply so many as are here wanting. And if there be fewer, the overplus may be omitted; Provided that this last Collect, Epistle and Gospel, shall always be used upon the Sunday next before Advent".

The reform of the Roman Calendar altered all this. As a result of this reform, on the Monday after the first Sunday after Epiphany, sometimes in England called Plough Monday, as it marked a return to work, there begins *tempus per annum*, which continues till the day before Ash Wednesday; it is resumed on the day after Pentecost and continued till the day before Advent Sunday. *Tempus per annum*, which literally means "time through the year", is translated "Ordinary Time", which seems to undervalue it in a way not intended by the Latin. Nevertheless this innovation does raise a question of principle. It used to be argued that the periods after Epiphany and after Trinity (or after Pentecost) were to some extent still under the influence of the preceding festivals; thus the idea of the incarnation continued to influence the Sundays after Epiphany, and this was borne out by the Gospels which both the Roman and the Anglican tradition used to have for the first two Sundays after Epiphany, namely the visit of Jesus as a boy to Jerusalem, and the miracle at Cana, which deal with beginnings rather than endings. The theory is less plausible when applied to the Sundays after Trinity, but reference can be made to Pentecost, and they can be described as Sundays concerning the Christian life in the Spirit.

Now, however, Pentecost is seen not as starting a season, but as concluding the Greaty Fifty Days, the Paschal Season. This incidentally has its disadvantages. If attention turns immediately after Ascension Day to the Holy Spirit, then Ascensiontide is diminished, and valuable material which might well be used on the Sunday after Ascension is lost. However that may be, the effect of the introduction of

Ordinary Time is to deprive the periods after Epiphany and after Trinity of any seasonal character. In the new Roman calendar there are thirty-four such weeks, and readings are normally provided for both their Sundays and their week-days. The first such week lacks its opening Sunday, for the first Sunday after Epiphany is the feast of the Baptism of the Lord, and the Ordinary Time starts on the Monday, but the next Sunday, which is strictly speaking the first Sunday to fall in the Ordinary Time, is called *Dominica II per annum*, for it is the Sunday of the second week of the Ordinary Time. No doubt it is popularly known as the second Sunday of Ordinary Time. The Solemnity of Christ the King, previously at the end of October, now replaces the Sunday at the beginning of the thirty-fourth and last week. Not every year, however, needs thirty-four ordinary weeks. The weeks after Epiphany always start as we have described and include the old pre-Lent Sundays before Ash Wednesday, but this whole period varies in length before it breaks off at Ash Wednesday. When the Ordinary Time is resumed on the Monday after Pentecost, it is resumed at such a point that the thirty-fourth week is always reached just before Advent. This will mean in some years that a week is omitted. Moreover Pentecost itself takes the place of the Sunday of the week in which Ordinary Time is resumed, and Trinity Sunday takes the place of the following Sunday.

CL has a somewhat similar scheme but with an important difference. The first five Sundays after Epiphany are so named and have, broadly speaking, the same lessons as the new Roman lectionary, so that the difference in the names is unimportant. But at the 6th Sunday after Epiphany the readings are described as Proper 1, at the 7th as Proper 2, at the 8th as Proper 3. The Last Sunday after Epiphany in CL is the Transfiguration. As the number of Sundays in this period varies, it is clear that in some years some or all of these Propers will not be reached. The Propers are not resumed till the Sunday after Trinity Sunday. In CL, as in the new Roman Calendar, the Propers are resumed at such a point that the last of them, Proper 29 in CL, always falls just before Advent. This is secured by labelling these Propers with actual dates; thus Proper 4 is to be used on the

Sunday between May 29 and June 4 inclusive, though only if this falls after Trinity Sunday. The Propers will start, at the latest, at Proper 8. They will not often start before Proper 4, but if Easter is very early, they may do so. CL therefore has this instruction: "If the Sunday between May 24 and 28 inclusive follows Trinity Sunday, use Eighth Sunday after Epiphany on that day". In other words, Proper 3 (and only that Proper) is available either after Epiphany or after Trinity. The result of this is of course that in some years Propers 4 to 7 may not be used. This arrangement is said by CL to bring the table into week-to-week conformity with the Roman system.

We now explain the probable reason why CL started the numbering of the Propers after Epiphany at such a point as to bring the resumption after Pentecost at Propers 3 to 8. This method gives the same numbering of the Propers as is used by *The Book of Common Prayer* of the (American) Episcopal Church, which has Proper 3 at "The Sunday closest to May 25". Its Propers 1 and 2, however, are not used after Epiphany as they are in CL, but if Easter is early, they are used for the weekdays after Pentecost and after Trinity Sunday; they are never used on a Sunday.

The Roman system has this advantage over CL. In the Roman system only one week of Ordinary Time, at most, is lost at the resumption after Pentecost. In CL if Easter is early, most of the Sundays after Epiphany, including Propers 1–3, are lost; if Easter is late, several of the Propers 4–7 are lost. On the other hand, this enables more passages to be set down in the Lectionary, even though they may be used but rarely.

JLG, however, has also altered the traditional year. It starts the year with five Sundays of what may be called pre-Advent. Ignoring for this purpose Epiphany, it contains the Sundays after Christmas to the point which the Sundays after Epiphany need to reach; that is, they break off at the old Septuagesima, the ninth Sunday before Easter. Thus JLG has nine Sundays before Christmas and nine before Easter. At the end of the year the Sundays after Pentecost, of course, break off five Sundays earlier than they used to do, in order to make way for pre-Advent, which begins at the ninth Sunday before Christmas. JLG knows nothing of the system of numbered propers. It was, however, designed in the expectation that there would soon be a fixed Easter; in the meantime certain lessons are provided for Extra Sundays after Christmas and Extra Sundays after Pentecost.

The users of JLG, however, have for the most part retained the traditional method of reckoning the Sundays after Epiphany, using the lessons for the third Sunday after Christmas on the first Sunday after Epiphany and so on (see p. 104). This raises no problem, so long as it is realised that in some years the second Sunday after Christmas has to be omitted. We shall henceforth consider JLG in this modified form.

Having thus described the very considerable discrepancies, which all interlock with each other, we now ask what can be done to reconcile them. We begin with the question raised by the JLG's five Sundays of pre-Advent: when is the Christian year to begin? There are ancient precedents for fasts of varying length in preparation for Christmas, and the purpose of this innovation, made by the JLG Calendar, was to meet the requirements of the JLG Lectionary, that is to enable the controlling lessons, which at this time are from the Old Testament, to proceed from Creation onwards, a sort of Easter Vigil spread over the Sundays. Four weeks would not suffice for this (see p. 101). This extended "run-up" to Christmas is a most valuable feature of JLG which many of its users would be reluctant to abandon, and it enables important Old Testament passages to be seen in their own light, though of course accompanied by suitable New Testament passages.

If, however, it is strongly felt that Advent Sunday must be regarded as the first Sunday of the Christian year, then it would be possible to regard the pre-Advent Sundays as the close of the previous year. Indeed the themes of beginning and ending are inextricably mixed up both in pre-Advent and in Advent. What used to be the Sunday next before Advent had a somewhat eschatological character, and so has the Roman and CL Solemnity of Christ the King, which falls on the same day. Advent itself, while looking forward to the celebration of Christ's birth, is yet concerned

with eschatological themes such as judgement. There is perhaps profound significance in the fact that when events
which occurred in a lineal sequence are represented by an
annual cycle, the end and the beginning are, as it were,
intertwined. This reminds us that there is a certain inevitable artificiality in the cyclic representation of lineal events,
admirable as that is. It also enables us to use the devotional
language which marked the expectation of Christ's first
coming to express our expectation of his final coming (see
p. 102).

The adoption by CL of the system of propers makes it
much easier to reconcile JLG to CL in the pre-Advent
season than it would have been to reconcile JLG to the traditional calendar. All that is needed is to say that the ninth
Sunday before Christmas corresponds to the Sunday of
Proper 25, and so on.

What then, is to be done with the Solemnity of Christ the
King, which falls on CL's Proper 29 and JLG's Fifth Sunday before Advent? Some might regard it as superfluous;
Ascension Day in a sense marks Christ's Kingship. But, if it
were desired, JLG could easily be adapted to it. As is
noted elsewhere (p. 114), the users of JLG have with vir-
tual unanimity altered the sequence by omitting the Sunday originally devoted to Noah, moving Abraham and
Moses forward a week, and filling the gap on the 5th
Sunday before Christmas by inserting The Remnant of
Israel. The readings now customarily used on this day have
their merits but were obviously not chosen by JLG; so it
would be possible to replace them, at least optionally, by
the CL readings for Christ the King without further disturbing the sequence.

The difficulties begin again at the Sunday after Epiphany
1. In CL this is bound to be Epiphany 2, but if Easter is very
early, JLG (as modified) will break off the Epiphany series
because it has reached the Ninth Sunday before Easter.
Sooner or later JLG will usually break off while CL goes
on; only when Easter is very late will the total number of
Sundays between Epiphany and Ash Wednesday be
required. If Easter is early, JLG will lose the lessons of some
of the Sundays after Epiphany, from the 2nd to the 6th, but

CL will lose later ones from the 4th to the 8th, the 9th being always retained by CL as the Transfiguration. There is no simple way of reconciling this difference. One side, however, could give way to the other as regards the *names* of the Sundays, while retaining its present choice of lessons. Thus JLG could agree to describe the ninth to the seventh Sundays before Easter as Sundays after Epiphany, whatever their numbering turned out to be in any given year, but with the proviso that on the last three of these Sundays after Epiphany the lessons now ascribed to the three pre-Lent Sundays would be read. This is no more illogical than the old Prayer Book provision for the Sunday next before Advent or indeed than CL's provision for the last Sunday after Epiphany. Conversely, CL could agree to describe the last three Sundays of its present Epiphany season as the Ninth to the Seventh Sundays before Easter, but with the proviso that they should retain their present readings.

The Transfiguration is a problem. Traditionally it is observed on August 6th, as it may still be. The new Roman lectionary, like the old, without giving any special name to the Sunday, has the appropriate readings on the second Sunday in Lent; CL has moved them to what it called Last Sunday after Epiphany (Transfiguration). CL argues that, just as the Sundays after Pentecost are completed with the Festival of Christ the King, so the Sundays after Epiphany should have such a climax. The CL table of lessons, however, allows alternative gospels on the second Sunday in Lent for those churches which wish to maintain the tradition of reading a Transfiguration gospel on that Sunday. JLG has Transfiguration lessons on the fourth Sunday in Lent, in their chronological place between the events at Caesarea Philippi and the approach to the Passion narrative. These questions about lessons, however, strictly speaking affect the calendar only, because CL uses the word "Transfiguration" as part of the name of a Sunday.

Passiontide presents a minor problem. It has been traditional to regard the fifth Sunday in Lent, sometimes called Passion Sunday, as introducing two weeks of Passiontide, sometimes called respectively Passion Week and Holy Week. JLG accordingly uses the names "2nd before Easter

(Passion)" and "1st before Easter (Palm)". The modern Roman usage has shortened this season to a week, so that the old Passion Sunday is simply the fifth Sunday in Lent, and the old Palm Sunday is described somewhat confusingly as "*Dominica in Palmis de Passione Domini*", translated "Passion Sunday (Palm Sunday)". This does, however, bring out the twofold character of the day, in which it is traditional to deal with the Palm Sunday entry into Jerusalem in a preliminary part of the service and to read a Passion narrative at the main service. CL to some extent follows the new Roman usage; the old Passion Sunday is split into alternatives. One set of readings is provided for what is called "Lent 6 when observed as Passion Sunday" and others for what is called "Lent 6 when observed as Palm Sunday". It would be simpler to call it Palm Sunday whatever the readings used.

The problems after Pentecost are more complicated. The CL Sundays have no names. A Sunday can hardly be described as (say) "The Sunday of Proper 6". In that respect the expression (say) "The twelfth Sunday of the ordinary time" or "The twelfth Sunday of the year" would be better, though the latter is confusing to those unversed in liturgical calendars, who would naturally count the Sundays of the year from January 1st onwards. It would thus seem best to retain the names "after Pentecost" whatever lessons are read. The question would still arise whether to follow the JLG method of simply starting the lesson series with certain lessons for Pentecost 2, and so on, till the series breaks off, or to follow the CL method of resuming the propers at a point most easily ascertained by reference to the secular calendar. In either case this season runs on till it breaks off at the start of the next Christian year, whether that be pre-Advent or Advent.

This raises one final problem. JLG, designed for a fixed Easter, was meant to come to a climax at Pentecost 20, "Citizens of Heaven". If Easter had been fixed, then Pentecost 21 would have been reached only very rarely. As it is, a whole range of Sundays may turn out to be the last. It would be an appropriate modification of JLG to lay down by a rubric that the lessons of Pentecost 20 should always be read on the last, even if this meant that the lessons of some Sundays would be omitted, or that the lessons of Pentecost 21, and possibly also of the Extra Sundays after Pentecost, would fill a gap till the last Sunday was reached.

To sum up: there are only minor problems about Advent, Christmastide, Lent and Eastertide; JLG's pre-Advent Sundays will also correspond with the Sundays having certain propers, but it is impossible to relate them to the numbering of the Sundays after Pentecost; there is no problem about the start of the Sundays after Epiphany, but the pre-Lent Sundays cannot be related to the numbering of the Sundays after Epiphany; and the Sundays after Pentecost cannot be related to particular propers. Only when decisions are made about the choices thus presented can progress be made about actual lessons. Yet the desire to have certain sequences of lessons inevitably affects the shape of the calendar.

11

LECTIONARY – WHY?

✠

David Beckett

An eighteenth-century minister of the City Temple is on record as having announced a four-month series of Sunday sermons on the mystical meaning of each colour in Joseph's coat.

This is why the church requires a lectionary.

The most obvious and basic value of a systematic calender of Bible readings (whatever the period of time covered by a particular lectionary's cycle) is that it helps to safeguard congregations from the most fanciful notions of those leading worship. It cannot be a substitute for disciplined and honest effort to expound the Word of God, a task which requires from the preacher humble and prayerful openness to the word he or she is privileged to impart; but congregations whose services are linked to a lectionary will generally be spared the worst effects of a minister's selectivity and subjectivity. Ministers willing to submit themselves to the discipline of preaching from a lectionary, inevitably having to grapple sometimes with difficult or uncongenial passages, will find reassurance in knowing that they are not cutting them or labouring their own private hobby-horses.

The churches which departed at the Reformation from the principle of calendar and lectionary were no doubt inspired by high ideals. The aim of celebrating the entire gospel every Lord's Day is an admirable one, but it is hardly practicable. If it is acknowledged that there is value in emphasising certain facets of the gospel at particular seasons (the Nativity at Christmas, Our Lord's death and resurrection at Easter, the gift of the Spirit at Pentecost) there can be no valid argument in principle against relating the story of the world's redemption to the progress of the calendar. Christmas carols and the record of Bethlehem are in theory just as relevant in July as in December; the Holy Spirit given to the church at Pentecost is a gift to be marvelled at in October as much as in May; but all churches find value in celebrating these big truths together at particular seasons, to take account of congregations' expectations and the annual rhythm of their members' lives. There is no logical reason why the sharing of big festivals should not be extended to other emphases and patterns.

In an age of increasing ecumenical concern and witness, a shared lectionary clearly has considerable unifying potential. Perhaps just as important is the effect it can have in making congregations more aware that they are worshipping in company with others of their own denominations. Where worshippers are made aware of a lectionary being a governing factor in their worship, they are (possibly unconsciously) made simultaneously aware that others are using it too, which is an important step towards seeing the worship of each parish as participation in the worship of the whole church catholic.

The roots of the lectionary reach back to the Old Testament times. Solemn liturgical reading of the Law was something the Hebrews regarded as having been enjoined by Moses himself (Deuteronomy 31.9–13) and the first stage towards the development of a lectionary was the use of festival readings from Leviticus for Passover, New Year's Day and the Feast of Tabernacles. Later a cycle of Sabbath readings evolved, the Pentateuch being divided into 150 sections and read in its entirety every three years. Probably by 200 B.C. it was accepted custom to add a lesson from the prophets as a second reading. Scripture could be read publicly by any male Israelite, although precedence was given to any priest or Levite in the congregation, and an element of exposition seems to have been usual at an early stage. The liturgical nature of scripture reading in Synagogue worship is reflected in the rule that neither reading nor exposition was permitted if fewer than ten men were present.

The church took over this established Hebrew custom of reading and expounding scripture in its worship. The Christian lectionary like its Jewish predecessor developed slowly, with considerable local variation. Much remains uncertain about this process, but it seems likely that some kind of continuous reading was used except at festivals. The use of a Psalm as a gradual between readings can be traced to an early stage in Christian history.

In synagogue worship and in the church until the sixteenth century, part of the lectionary's function was to present the scriptures to people who depended on public worship for any knowledge of the Bible. Nowadays the effect of lectionary prescriptions may be rather different. Far from opening up new vistas, the rotation of a relatively small selection of key biblical material may foster the impression that the lectionary covers "the important bits" and that passages not listed in this digest are by implication not significant. This is a danger for denominations which may feel that they are opening up the scriptures to their people by providing just a lectionary for Sunday services. The resources of the Bible are so vast that Sunday readings, whether on a two- or three-year cycle, must have limitations if not supplemented by a daily calendar. In churches whose public worship is commonly limited to one service per week, the benefits of knowing that key themes and subjects are being regularly dealt with will be largely offset by the uncomfortable knowledge that large portions of the scriptures are never being used at all. The problem here is not the inadequacy of a lectionary so much as the hopelessness of trying to do justice to the scriptures and fulfil a teaching ministry on the basis of one hour a week; although it is arguable that congregations in this situation are likely to receive a richer diet when a lectionary is used than when it is not used.

A lectionary then can offer certain safeguards to a congregation and a helpful discipline to preachers. It can help in achieving solidarity between congregations and in building bridges between different denominations. It has an authentic place in the tradition of biblical worship, reaching further back in time than the New Testament itself. Some branches of the church though would make much stronger claims for it than these – believing that the lectionary worked out and ratified by church authority becomes part of the "given-ness" of worship, an integral part of the celebration of the people of God. The introduction, for example, to the readings in *The New Sunday Missal* begins "Over the period of three years the Church unfolds the gospels to us Sunday by Sunday". This emphasis which assumes the provision of scriptural materials for congregations by "the Church" is different from the tone of the commendation of the lectionary in the American Presbyterian *Worshipbook*: "Presbyterians are not required to follow a lectionary as they plan for worship on the Lord's Day. On the other hand, the following of a lectionary, with flexibility, helps assure a congregation that it will not, in the course of a period of years, neglect the great teachings of the Bible" – a more modest, though from some perspectives much more negative, view of the place a lectionary has in the church's worship. Roman Catholics and Anglicans would affirm that the lectionary should be seen as something more than just a syllabus for preaching. Within the Reformed tradition there would be unease over the Roman distinction between The Church which provides the lectionary and the worshipping congregation which receives it.

Discussions within the Joint Liturgical Group revealed that this difference in emphasis extends also to the relationship in how worship should respond to events in the life of the world. There are occasions when congregations gather in the hope of hearing some word that is pertinent to a local disaster, a national celebration or crisis, or a recent turn in world events. Without conceding the right of ministers habitually to cull their sermons from the daily papers, most Protestant and Reformed preachers would cherish the freedom to turn aside on occasion from the lectionary prescription to meet the demands of a particular situation. To do otherwise would smack of unacceptable liturgical fundamentalism, and the interruption of the lectionary would generally be regarded as less damaging than severing the unity of the Word read and proclaimed. In churches which regard the lectionary as vitally important for its own sake there is not the same feeling that the preaching must relate to what has been read. The sermon may set forth the Word in the context of current happenings in the world. The readings set forth the unfolding drama of God's mighty acts within the world.

12

THE JLG LECTIONARY

✠

A. Raymond George

JLG in the Statement issued by its first meeting on 10–11 October, 1963 listed three initial projects which it had decided to discuss. The first was "The planning of a Calendar, Forms of Daily Service, and a Lectionary which the Churches might be glad to have in common". In 1967 they published *The Calendar and Lectionary: A Reconsideration* (O.U.P.), in 1968 *The Daily Office* (SPCK and Epworth) and in 1969 *An Additional Lectionary for use at a Second Sunday Service* (SPCK and Epworth). Reference will be made later to the revision of *The Daily Office* and to the two editions of *Holy Week Services*.

It would theoretically have been possible to prepare and publish these simultaneously, but priority was given to the lectionary for the main Sunday service by publishing first *The Calendar and Lectionary*. Four other days were added to the body of the lectionary, viz: Christmas Day (for which two sets of lessons were provided, presumably one for use at midnight and the other for the day itself), Ash Wednesday, Good Friday and Ascension Day. A note made provision "if Epiphany is celebrated on 6 January".

Clearly the lectionary is dependent on the calendar, but some of the innovations in the calendar were made to suit the requirements of the proposed lectionary.

A chapter by Neville Clark expounded the principles of the lectionary. As he pointed out, some church traditions have three services – Mattins, Eucharist, Evensong. Others have two – Morning Worship and Evening Worship with Holy Communion periodically connected with one or the other or both. It might be added that where there are three services, the church can to some extent be divided into those which lay the greater emphasis on Mattins and those which lay it on the Eucharist. JLG decided to concentrate on what Clark called "the liturgical lectionary, designed for the Service of the Word and Sacrament; or for a Service which, though the Sacrament is not celebrated, follows the same order".

Given this task to produce a lectionary for such a service on Sundays and four other special days based on a revised calendar, two further questions remain. How many lessons are required for such a service? Over what period should the lectionary extend?

The general custom of the churches had long been to have two lessons at a service: Old Testament and New Testament at Mattins and Evensong or Morning and Evening Worship, and Epistle (or occasionally some other passage in place of the Epistle) and Gospel at the Eucharist, at least in those churches which followed a eucharistic lectionary. It was decided to have three: Old Testament, Epistle (occasionally Acts or Revelation) and Gospel. Though the Epistles and the Gospels alike bear witness to the new covenant in Christ, they do so by very different methods, and it seems fitting that the special witness of the Gospels to the incarnate life of Christ should always be available. It was strongly urged that all three lessons should be read, but it is open to any denomination adopting this lectionary to indicate how it is to be used, e.g. by indicating that either the Old Testament reading or the Epistle may be omitted. When three readings are provided, they tend to be rather shorter than when there are only two. The total provision is about thirty verses each Sunday. In order to meet the requirement of longer readings by those churches which use only two, provision was made for some of the Old Testament readings to be optionally lengthened; there were longer and shorter versions. The wisdom of providing three, however, was confirmed by the decision of the Roman Catholic Church also to provide three readings on Sundays. The Roman revision took place at about the same time, and unfortunately there was little contact between the

98

Roman revisers and JLG until each party had gone too far to withdraw. This, however, makes the agreement on this point all the more striking.

As the calendar covers only one year, it might seem that the lectionary should do the same, as had been traditional in many churches. But this is not adequate for what Clark called "the rich sweep of Scripture". A two-year cycle was therefore planned. The Romans at the same time were planning a three-year cycle, which has certain advantages. It may be felt, however, that a two-year interval is long enough before hearing again the greatest scriptural passages. A cycle of even more than three years would begin to undermine the whole concept of a fixed lectionary.

The major problem to be faced is, however, whether the lessons should be continuous or thematic. Continuous reading (lectio continua) forms part of many church traditions. It is obviously most appropriate for a daily office, and was indeed followed subsequently in JLG's *The Daily Office*. It could also be defended for use on Sundays, at least in a modified form.

A two-year cycle provides more than a hundred Gospel readings, more than there are chapters in the Gospels, but as most of the chapters are far too long to constitute one lesson, there would clearly have to be many omissions. In the Old Testament the volume of material makes continuous reading virtually impossible in a Sunday lectionary. There is the further disadvantage that if each of two or three series of readings proceeds continuously, they will not bear any relation to one another. The principle would probably be modified by making one series, presumably the Gospels, continuous or semi-continuous, and then fitting the other series to it, thus adopting to some extent the thematic principle. The Roman Sunday lectionary has in this way chosen Old Testament lessons to fit the semi-continuous Gospel series, but this accentuates the fact that the Epistle is then "the odd man out".

The thematic principle has the great advantage that the readings for any one Sunday all deal with the same subject, a great advantage for preachers who can refer to all three and explain their relation. Even the most ardent supporters of the continuous principle must allow exceptions for such special days as Easter Day; why should not this obvious advantage be available every Sunday? It is open, however, to the criticism that the fixing of the themes seems somewhat arbitrary and subjective; lectionary-makers are tempted to ride their own hobby-horses, especially in the long weeks after Pentecost or Trinity. Moreover some very good lessons may be omitted because they do not fit well under any of the themes. JLG claims, however, that it has used a third method. The primary aim is to let Scripture speak and impose its own terms. It is to give place to the totality of biblical revelation in all the diversity of its witness. In the first part of the Christian year the calendar, itself based on the biblical revelation to some extent, imposes the choice of lessons; in the period after Pentecost the lectionary-maker is more free. In the first part of the year certain major festivals such as Christmas, Epiphany, Easter, Ascension, and Pentecost are based on passages in the Gospels or, in the case of Pentecost, on Acts 2; and certain other days such as Palm Sunday and Easter 1 are also related to events recorded in the Gospels. In the period after Pentecost, attention naturally turns to the history of the early Church and to the Christian life in the Holy Spirit, and this requires emphasis on lessons from Acts and the Epistles. Thus it was decided first to choose "controlling lessons" and then to choose others which would support them. If only two lessons are read, the controlling lessons should not be omitted. The controlling lessons from Christmas to the verge of Pentecost would be from the Gospels and would deal with our Lord's birth, life, ministry, Passion, resurrection and ascension. The controlling lessons after Pentecost would be from Acts and the Epistles. This leaves the four Sundays of Advent and the whole of the Old Testament. It is appropriate that controlling lessons from the Old Testament should prepare the way for Christmas, but the four Sundays of Advent are insufficient. This is the point at which the proposals for the lectionary influenced the calendar. The pre-Christmas period was lengthened from four Sundays to nine, and the controlling lessons began on the ninth Sunday before Christmas at the beginning of Genesis. There was some ancient precedent for a pre-Christmas fast of more than four weeks, and A. A. McArthur of the Church of Scotland in *The Evolution of the Christian Year* (SCM 1953) and *The Christian Year and Lectionary Reform* (SCM 1958) had advocated a somewhat similar scheme and worked it out in detail in his Peterhead lectionary. Moreover the use of nine Sundays gives the same number of Sundays to prepare for Christmas as there are to prepare for Easter. The themes for the ninth to the fifth Sundays before Christmas were: The Creation, The Fall, The Covenant of Preservation: Noah, The Election of God's People: Abraham, The Promise of Redemption: Moses. These five pre-Advent weeks raise an important question: how far can an Old Testament controlling lesson really dominate a Christian service? The problem is particularly acute on the Sunday devoted to the Fall. The preacher's message cannot be "Today I am telling you that you are fallen sinners, but if you will persist in coming till Christmas, you will then hear the beginning of the story of redemption". There is a sense in which the theme of every Christian service, whatever the lessons chosen or theme stated, is simply the Gospel of Christ. Nevertheless the good news of Christ has various aspects, which need to be brought out unless the sermon is to be always the same; and the provision of Epistle and Gospel fitting the Old Testament lessons brings this out. Thus on the Fall Sunday in the first year, the Gospel includes John 3:16, one of the most comforting and evangelical texts in the whole Bible. Yet the preacher on this Sunday may well start from the Fall story; for if it is never mentioned in the preaching, a congregation will tend to forget its significance and to lack guidance in its interpretation. Similarly the themes later in the year which might be described as ethical, such as the Neighbour or the Family, are to be related to the fundamental offer of the Gospel.

It might be expected that the series of controlling lessons from the Old Testament would continue in the four Advent Sundays through the Old Testament books in roughly their biblical order, but this is only partly achieved. In the first year, all four readings are from Isaiah. The fact is that the traditional Advent themes have prevailed, and the basic notion of JLG has had to give way to it. Advent itself and especially Advent 1 has in any case a mixture of traditional themes: expectation both of the first coming of Christ and of his final coming. The Old Testament lesson deals with the former, the New Testament lessons with the latter. Christian liturgy and hymnody use the language appropriate to the Old Testament expectation in order to express both their longing for Christmas, though of course Christ has already come, and their hope for his final triumph.

> O come, O come, Emmanuel
> And ransom captive Israel.

Advent 2 has in the first year the traditional Epistle, Romans 15.4–13, which, in introducing a number of Old Testament quotations of a forward-looking nature, refers to the purpose of Holy Scripture. The Prayer Book contains a collect based on that verse, and thus in countries influenced by Anglicanism it became Bible Sunday. JLG ingeniously retained this emphasis but relates it to the dominance of the Old Testament lessons in this season by stating the theme as "The Word of God in the Old Testament".

Advent 3 in the Prayer Book has passages related to the Advent ordinations: 1 Corinthians 4.1–5 deals with ministry, and Matthew 11.2–10 views John the Baptist as preparing the way before Christ, using a quotation from Malachi 3.1. JLG has The Forerunner as the theme, meaning John the Baptist, and has Malachi 3.1–5 and Matthew 11.2–15 as the readings for the second year. For the Epistle it has Philippians 4.4–9, in which the words "The Lord is at hand" are appropriate to the general Advent theme; this Epistle has sometimes been used on Advent 3 and sometimes on Advent 4. Its use on Advent 3 harmonizes with the traditional name of the Sunday, *Gaudete*, Rejoice, the first word of the traditional Introit. The first year's readings are 1 Corinthians 4.1–5, the traditional passage on ministry, together with another account of John the Baptist, John 1.19–27, which, together with one more verse, is the Prayer

Book Gospel for the following Sunday; the Old Testament lesson is Isaiah 40.1–11, which is suitable to Advent in general and contains a verse quoted in the John passage. This Sunday is a good example of the skilful use of traditional material within the JLG framework, but the description of the Isaiah and Malachi passages as the controlling lessons is rather artificial. The real control is exercised by the Gospels. Though the incidents described occur during Christ's lifetime, John the Baptist deserves a Sunday to himself, and it is sensible to put this before Christmas. His own birthday is traditionally observed on 24 June.

This early use of some of the material traditionally associated with Advent 4 leaves that Sunday free for another theme: The Annunciation. This is traditionally observed on 25 March, nine months before Christmas, but such feasts are not much observed in the Church of Scotland and in the Free Churches. Indeed they cause some difficulty in Roman and Anglican churches, particularly when they fall in Lent, or just before or even on Easter Day or just after it.

It is very appropriate that the Annunciation should be remembered just before Christmas. Indeed the account of it in Luke 1.26–38 is usually read in the Service of Nine Lessons at Christmastide. Moreover, the modern custom is to sing carols in the weeks *before* Christmas; the festival is in danger of being altogether anticipated: congregations want a decided air of Christmas in their services, and this theme goes some way to meet that demand. Still more does the Gospel in the second year, Matthew 1.18–23, which is an angelic announcement to Joseph: it stops just short of the actual birth. As on the previous Sunday, it is an artificial device to regard the Old Testament passages as the controlling lessons.

Christmas Day is straightforward. The Gospels are now the controlling lessons and all the readings are so obviously appropriate that the second year does not differ from the first. Provision is made for two services.

The period after Christmas raises as many problems as Advent. The Western tradition is to hold back the wise men till Epiphany on 6 January, but popular piety knows nothing of these fine distinctions, and carols referring to the

Wise Men are often sung even before Christmas. Moreover 6th January is not a public holiday or a popular festival, and for Methodists it has the further disadvantage that if it falls on a Sunday, that is the Sunday, the first in the New Year, on which the Covenant Service is usually held. It therefore seemed right to JLG to have Matthew 2.1–12 on Christmas 1, and to make the Wise Men the theme. Not all churches have followed this suggestion.

Epiphany itself does not appear in the body of the JLG Lectionary, but, as already mentioned, a note provides lessons "if Epiphany is celebrated on 6 January". Anyone following JLG literally would have almost the same lessons on two successive Sundays when Epiphany falls on a Sunday, if the Epiphany readings are preferred to those of Christmas 2, but a church can provide, by a suitable rubric, for the avoidance of this difficulty, as by exchanging in such a year the readings for Christmas 1 and 2. A more serious difficulty is that the JLG Calendar continues the numbering of the Sundays after Christmas, whereas traditionally the numbering starts afresh after Epiphany. Generally speaking, the churches have not followed JLG's lead; even churches which hardly observe 6 January at all nevertheless observe the tradition. This would not matter if there were a simple equivalence, so that Epiphany 1 would always be Christmas 3. But sometimes there is only one Sunday after Christmas before Epiphany; therefore those who adopt the JLG lectionary to the traditional calendar, so that the Sundays after Epiphany have always the same readings, must in some years omit the readings for Christmas 2.

Christmas 2 begins the narration of the events which followed Christ's birth and the Epiphany to the Wise Men, viz. Luke 2.21–40 and Luke 2.41–52, the themes being The Presentation in the Temple and The Visit to Jerusalem; the Prayer Book has the latter on Epiphany 1. This is the first of a number of Sundays when the first and second years have different themes. The presentation is traditionally observed on 2 February, but as with other feasts which often fall on weekdays, it was wise to allot it to a Sunday, at least in alternate years.

Thereafter the Gospels deal with Christ's adult life and

ministry. Tradition, especially in the East, regards the Epiphany as including within itself commemoration of the Baptism and of the wedding at Cana; the Prayer Book omits the former from the eucharistic Gospels and has the latter on Epiphany 2. The JLG lectionary has the former on Christmas 3 (which resembles the modern Roman practice of having it on Epiphany 1) and the latter on Christmas 5, first year. (It has often been the practice in the past for churches which observe 6 January when falling on a weekday to make a good deal of the Wise Men on Epiphany 1, and indeed Epiphany used to have an octave in the Roman rite. This would now diminish the importance of the Baptism, and is an additional argument in favour of making the Wise Men the theme of Christmas 1.) Meanwhile JLG has The First Disciples on Christmas 4; Gospels are the controlling lessons, but the Epistle and the equivalent from *Acts* have by coincidence the advantage that they fall somewhere near 25 January, the traditional date for the Conversion of St. Paul, to which they refer. The notion of "first" is then continued on Christmas 5 where the theme is stated as The First Sign: (1st year) The Wedding at Cana, (2nd year) The New Temple. The words "The First Sign" refer directly to the first-year passage which in John 2.11 uses the phrase "the first of his signs". After this Christmas 6 has passages from the earlier chapters of the Gospels, proclaiming the Lord whether as the Friend of Sinners or as Life for the World. There is not enough provision for the Sundays after Christmas, because it was hoped that a fixed Easter would soon be established; the lack has to be supplied from readings for Extra Sundays after Christmas, for which no theme is given.

This series breaks off in order to start the Easter cycle at the 9th Sunday before Easter. The movement is no longer away from Christmas, but towards Easter. Just as the preparation for Christmas now consists of five Sundays before Advent and then four Sundays in Advent, so the preparation for Easter has long consisted of three Sundays of Pre-Lent, and six Sundays of Lent, nine in all in each case. Pre-Lent has typical passages from Christ's ministry depicting Christ as teacher (and many churches now observe this as Education Sunday), Healer, and Worker of Miracles. Ash Wednesday has lessons on penitence and fasting, though no theme is stated. The first five Sundays of Lent all have themes beginning The King and the Kingdom, which holds them to some extent together; the Kingdom is of course a central theme of the ministry. The particular themes are stated as Temptation, Conflict, Suffering, Transfiguration, Victory of the Cross. Temptation is of course out of its chronological place, which is just after the Baptism at the beginning of Christ's ministry, but Lent, originally an immediate preparation for Easter, has long been connected also with Christ's forty days fasting and being tempted (Mark 1.13); this dislocation is inevitable, and the Kingdom of God is the true context of the Temptations. In the first year the traditional Gospel is lengthened to link the Temptation with the Kingdom. Conflict and Suffering refer to passages from the middle chapters of the Gospels; indeed Matthew 16.13–28, Caesarea Philippi, is something of a turning-point. Proceeding chronologically, we thus arrive on Lent 4 at Transfiguration, which tradition observes on 6 August, and the modern Roman rite on Lent 2. Lent 4 is traditionally Mothering Sunday, probably because of the occurrence of the words "mother" at Galatians 4.26 in the Prayer Book Epistle, but that passage has not been used here. A specifically Mothering Sunday service is perhaps best regarded as extra-liturgical, and not held at the usual hour of worship.

When Easter is but two weeks away, the season of Passiontide has traditionally begun, and this is reflected in the name Passion Sunday; modern Roman usage has cut the season to a week and very confusingly calls the following Sunday Passion Sunday (Palm Sunday). The Prayer Book, following ancient usage, has for the Epistle Hebrews 9.11–15a, a classic statement of the theology of the Passion, which JLG has adopted for the second year (adding verse 15b). For the Gospels it is too soon to start on the Passion-narratives; so passages have been chosen which point forward to the Passion, and such verses as John 12: 32 suggest the theme The Victory of the Cross. The Church on this Sunday looks forward, as it were, to the saving benefits of

106

Christ's Passion before becoming immersed in the historical details.

On Palm Sunday tradition suggests that the St. Matthew Passion should serve as the Gospel, and that the entry into Jerusalem should be commemorated in an act of Worship immediately before the main Service. JLG, however, followed a fairly widespread modern custom of prescribing the story of the entry as the Gospel, though with the Passion as a bracketed alternative, "on the assumption that the Passion narratives may be read throughout Holy Week". The reading of Zechariah 9.9–12 in the first year is also related to the entry. The theme given to the Sunday, The Way of the Cross, with its suggestion of movement along a road, subtly combines the two subjects.

Good Friday and Easter Day are of the greatest importance, but raise no particular problems. The Good Friday Passion narrative has longer and shorter forms. Easter Day, like Christmas Day, has provision for two services; and Good Friday and the second service for Easter Day, like both the services for Christmas Day, have identical provision in both years.

From Easter 1 to Easter 4 the two years diverge. The first year has a series of post-resurrection appearances; on Easter 1 the Gospel includes the appearance to Thomas, which according to John 20.26 occurred eight days after Easter. The Epistles treat of the final victory to which the resurrection points. The second year has a series of "I am" sayings from St. John's Gospel, including the Good Shepherd in its traditional place on Easter 2. They come before the resurrection in the Gospel narrative, but "As concentrating on the reality of life eternal, and as represented as coming from the lips of the Lord who is already, in some sense, conqueror of death, these passages are specially appropriate here".

Clark, whom we have again just quoted, makes no comment on Easter 5, but in fact the choice of two successive passages (one for each year) from John 16 (part of the farewell discourse), from which the Gospel of this Sunday is traditionally drawn, looks forward to the Ascension. The phrase "going to the Father" occurs at John 16.28 and is

107

given as the theme. It looks forward to the Ascension. The
Sunday, however, because it precedes the Rogation Days, is
sometimes known as Rogation Sunday and is devoted to
the theme of intercessory prayer, and John 16 fortunately
has teaching on this subject.

Ascension Day has the same readings in both years, and
the same theme is maintained on the following Sunday,
Easter 6, which has the same Gospel in both years.

The name Pentecost is preferred to Whitsunday. The
choice of controlling lesson is obvious, Acts 2.1–11, which
takes the place of the Epistle. This and the Gospel are the
same in both years; the Old Testament lessons are not the
same, but are both from Joel 2.

The controlling lessons in the second year are taken from
Acts 2 for two more Sundays, and from later chapters of
Acts for three more after that; in the first year the controlling lessons begin at once from the Epistles, and from
Pentecost 2 to Pentecost 6 a series of lessons from Exodus
and Deuteronomy shows that "as the Church moves forward from the Cross–Resurrection experience, so Israel
moved forward from the Exodus deliverance in pilgrimage
to the Promised Land" (Clark). The themes announced
vary between the two years. Thus on Pentecost 1 the first
year theme is The Riches of God; the second year theme is
The Church's Message. This is of course Trinity Sunday,
and it might have been simpler to have given the Holy
Trinity as the theme in both years. The word "Trinity",
however, does not occur in the Bible, and it seemed best to
let these lessons, with the supporting lessons, provide the
material out of which the doctrine of the Trinity was eventually constructed. Moreover, the Acts passage is part of a
series from Acts 2, and the Gospel for the first year is part
of a series of lessons from the Johannine farewell-discourse.
From Pentecost 6 onwards there is again but a single theme
for each Sunday.

Clark admits that it was tempting to adopt a thematic
approach for the post-Pentecost season where the Calendar
loosens its control. He insists, however, that this temptation
was resisted and the Bible was allowed to dictate its own
conclusion. Of course there was a subjective element in the

choice, but the passages are largely those selected by the Church through the ages. The controlling lessons (all from Acts or the Epistles apart from one from Revelation) were *first* selected and then arranged so that some general progression emerged. The thematic titles are only *indications* of emphasis. The supporting lessons usually deal to some extent with the same theme. But the theme must not dominate the mind of the preacher. The lessons say different things to different people, and he should let the lessons speak their own message to him. Nor need he confine his exposition to the controlling lesson. Often he may enrich his sermon, though probably based on one text, by explaining the connection between all three. Sometimes he may simply expound one, which may well be one of the supporting lessons. This is one of the answers to those critics of the lectionary who ask what is to be done when it comes round for a second time. *The Alternative Service Book 1980* was perhaps wise in hiding the themes away in an appendix. There are even purists who object to telling the congregation what the theme is before reading the lessons, though it will usually be found that a knowledge of the theme enables them to follow the lessons with greater appreciation.

From Pentecost 11 to Pentecost 13 there is a short series on the Church as a serving, witnessing and suffering community, and these marks of the Church are linked to the mission of God's ancient people by the use in the first year of three of the servant songs from the second part of Isaiah.

The post-Pentecost season was meant to come to a fitting conclusion at Pentecost 20, when a lesson reminiscent of All Saints Day suggested the theme Citizens of Heaven. Had Easter been fixed as was hoped, Pentecost 21 would have become necessary only when 22 October falls on a Sunday. In the absence of a fixed Easter, the extra Sundays after Pentecost have also often to be used.

In 1968 JLG published *The Daily Office*, probably the most successful of its books. It was brought out just in time for the Lambeth Conference of that year. Like the Sunday lectionary, it is on a two-yearly basis. It has for each day three lessons, and the full form of the office suggests Old Testament and Epistle (including Acts and Revelation) for the morning and Gospel for the evening. It is also suggested that the year not being used for the Office might be used for a daily Eucharist. The whole of the New Testament is read each year, and nearly the whole of the Old Testament once every two years. The books are read in Course, except for certain special weeks such as Holy Week. In the Old Testament, "track-reading" is employed; in other words, there are some omissions. The lectionary covers only weekdays, and an attempt has been made to fit the weekday lessons to the same pattern as the Sunday lectionary. This occasionally means that the readings for Monday overlap with those of the preceding Sunday.

The choice of books for the various seasons is thus dictated partly by the Sunday lectionary, partly by tradition. Thus the creation narratives on the ninth Sunday before Christmas start (in the first year) five weeks of reading from Genesis, though of course the Fall is passed on a weekday before it is reached on a Sunday. Advent follows tradition in using Isaiah and eschatological passages from the gospels, and Revelation is used in the first year both in pre-Advent and in Advent. Later in Advent the passages deal with Elijah and John the Baptist. Jeremiah is particularly appropriate for pre-Lent and Lent. After Easter the John passages in the second year harmonise with the Sunday readings, and it is suggested in the preliminary comments (this time anonymous) that readings from 1 Kings about the kingdom established by David may be thought appropriate during the season when the Church rejoices at the victory of David's greater Son. After Pentecost, selections from Numbers and Deuteronomy in the first year deal with the People of God.

Acts is obviously appropriate; it comes early in this period in one year and later in the other. Towards the end there are selections from the Apocrypha, with alternatives from the Old Testament. The Psalms were not included in the lectionary; the book contained a separate Psalter, which is not our concern here.

In 1978 JLG published *The Daily Office Revised with*

Other Prayers and Services. Though the Psalter was completely altered, the lessons were unchanged, except for very small details. The Epistles and Gospels were, however, switched about from time to time, so that in some weeks the Morning Office would have the Gospel and the Evening Office the Epistle. The comments and other passages which had made *The Daily Office* look like a draft for a committee (or indeed for the Lambeth Conference), rather than a devotional book, were omitted and replaced by other devotional material. It is to be regretted however, that the 1978 book does not contain the admirable 1968 introduction by S. F. Winward, a Baptist, explaining the use of an office, as well as the short *Introductory Essay* of 1978 by Gordon S. Wakefield, a Methodist.

In 1969 JLG published a small pamphlet, now probably difficult to obtain, *An Additional Lectionary for use at a Second Sunday Service.* It contains two lessons, Old Testament and New Testament, on a two-year cycle for all the Sundays assuming a fixed Easter (but with extra Sundays if needed), and Christmas Day (but not Epiphany), Ash Wednesday, Good Friday, and Ascension Day. As R. C. D. Jasper explained in a one-page introduction, the themes of the Eucharistic Lectionary are followed, though with some freedom and flexibility. The only major variation is that, in Lent till Passion Sunday, Mark's Passion-narrative is read in the first year and Luke's in the second. With very few exceptions, the passages from the Eucharistic Lectionary have been avoided; and on the four occasions where complete passages occur in both lectionaries, they are in different years. This inevitably gives rise to the thought that these passages are, so to speak, "the second team". If such invidious comparisons must be made, it is fitting that the principal service should have the best lessons. It is usually assumed that this will be in the morning, when congregations are in many places larger, but where the evening congregation is larger it is possible to reverse the two. Usually the congregation at a smaller second service consists of better instructed Christians, and they are better able to appreciate more difficult lessons. Moreover it is possible to follow strictly the Eucharistic Lectionary but to use the

111

second service for worship of a much freer kind, without the use of a lectionary. But the charge sometimes made, that JLG has quite overlooked certain important passages, is to some extent countered by the existence of this second lectionary, and those who do not use it will probably end up by using less of scripture than the two lectionaries, taken together, contain.

Holy Week Services (SPCK & Epworth, 1971) and *Holy Week Services*, Revised and expanded edition (SPCK, 1983) also contained lessons. We here describe the lessons in the latter, which differ only slightly from those in the original edition. On Palm Sunday, the accounts of the entry into Jerusalem are assigned to the beginning of the service, preceding the procession. The other lessons given in *The Calendar and Lectionary*, though no longer ascribed to particular years, are retained. Thus there is now no alternative to a Passion-narrative in the main service; this should discourage the practice whereby the entry into Jerusalem forms the theme of the entire service, with its unfortunate result that no Sunday in the year is devoted to the death of Christ. The St. Matthew Passion is, however, shortened, and yet a shorter alternative is provided. The St. Mark Passion appears as an alternative, also in two different lengths. Both Passions are set out, as also that for Good Friday, in a form suitable for the traditional style of dramatic reading.

JLG had not previously provided readings, apart from the readings for the office, for the first three weekdays of Holy Week. Each day has now two possible principal services; the first service for each day includes part of a Passion-narrative, in the first year from St. Mark, in the second year from St. Luke. On Tuesday Mark 14.2742 is presumably a misprint for 14.27–72, a mistake which occurs in both editions. These are the same gospels as were prescribed for the second Service for the first five Sundays of Lent. It would have been better to have crossed St. Mark and St. Luke over in one of these places. In the alternative service for each day, first introduced in the revised edition, the Gospels describe the events of the day, and the supporting lessons are chosen to fit.

Three themes are to be found in the lessons for Maundy

Thursday: the institution of the Eucharist, the footwashing (John 13.1–15), and the giving of the new commandment to love one another (John 13.34–35). It is the last of these which in English gives the day its name, *mandatum* being the Latin for commandment. JLG provides that "During the reading of the Gospel, following it, or at a later point in the service, the ceremony of the washing of the feet may take place". The gospel in the first year is John 13.1–15, the footwashing; in the second year it is Mark 14.12–26, the institution of the Eucharist; in that year the footwashing will obviously come *after* the gospel, and during it are read John 13.5, the core of the footwashing narrative, and John 13.34–35, the new commandment. Reference is made to the Eucharist in both years in the epistle; in the first year this is 1 Corinthians 11.23–29, Paul's account of the institution, and in the second year (when the gospel has Mark's account) some verses about the Eucharist from 1 Corinthians 10.16–17. Because the epistle is thus so closely connected with the Eucharist, it is recommended that it be read not in its usual place, though that is a permissible alternative, but just before the President takes the bread and wine and before the Thanksgiving Prayer is said.

On Good Friday there is no suggestion of a shorter version of St. John's Passion, as there was in *The Calendar and Lectionary*, and indeed even the longer version has been slightly lengthened. For the Old Testament lesson, Isaiah 52.13–53 end, has replaced Exodus 12.1–11, which was in *The Calendar and Lectionary*. This, in the form 12.1–8, 11–14, has been moved to Maundy Thursday, first year. This transposition is a considerable improvement.

The Easter Vigil has some of the traditional lessons, three from the Old Testament, and an Epistle and Gospel. It is not clear how these are related to the first set for Easter in *The Calendar and Lectionary*. The Vigil and the second year of that set have Matthew 28.1–10 in common; otherwise there is no substantial overlap, which leaves almost two complete sets for Easter Day itself.

JLG has thus sought to achieve its aim to let Scripture speak and impose its own terms.

We now trace briefly the use which the churches have

made of these proposals. The lessons in *The Calendar and Lectionary* have been widely adopted, e.g. in *The Methodist Service Book*, 1975 (*MSB*), *The Book of Common Order* (*1979*) (*BCO*), of the Church of Scotland, and, though with some alterations, in *A Book of Services*, 1980 (*BS*), of the United Reformed Church in England and Wales, and in *The Alternative Service Book 1980* (*ASB*) of the Church of England. One alternative has been made in all of these. Noah has been omitted; Abraham and Moses have been moved a week earlier, and the fifth Sunday before Christmas has 1 Kings 19.9–18; Romans 11.13–24; Matthew 24.37 (some have 38)–44 in the first year, and Isaiah 10.20–23; Romans 9.19–28 (some have 29) Mark 13.14–23 in the second year. The Theme is The Remnant of Israel, but *BCO* does not print themes.

ASB has made considerable changes in the Christmas and Epiphany season, as may be seen by looking at their list of themes. Christmas 1 has The Incarnation, and Christmas 2 The Holy Family. On the Sundays after Epiphany each theme begins with the word Revelation, and then there follow on the six Sundays respectively The Baptism of Jesus, The first Disciples, Signs of Glory, The New Temple, The Wisdom of God, Parables. *BS* is roughly similar, but there are slight variations.

BCO, keeping to the JLG lessons, and *BS* taking the *ASB* variations, do not start numbering the Sundays afresh after Epiphany, but continue with Christmas 3, 4 etc. *MSB*, keeping to the JLG lessons, and *ASB*, with its variations, have Epiphany 1–6. This can lead to much confusion in years when there is only one Sunday after Christmas before Epiphany. In such years *MSB* and *ASB* will celebrate The Baptism of Jesus on Epiphany 1, but *BCO* and *BS* on Christmas 3, which will be Epiphany 2; and so on. JLG's Extra Sundays after Christmas, put in by JLG for use until we have a fixed date for Easter, are handled in various ways.

On the 7th Sunday before Easter *ASB* and *BS* have replaced Christ, Worker of Miracles, by Christ the Friend of Sinners, brought there from Christmas 6 (1st year).

At Pentecost 14–16 *ASB* and *BS* have altered the order of

114

The Neighbour, The Family, Those in Authority, to The Family, Those in Authority, The Neighbour.

At the end of the season after Pentecost, the question of the Extra Sundays is again variously handled. *ASB* and *BS* always have Citizens of Heaven (*JLG*'s Pentecost 20) on the Last Sunday after Pentecost, whichever that may be.

In a number of cases *ASB* and *BS*, while retaining the themes, have altered some of the lessons.

An Additional Lectionary for use at a Second Sunday Service has not been widely followed, but *MSB* reproduced it almost exactly, making its own adjustment in order to deal with Noah and The Remnant of Israel.

13

THE ROMAN LECTIONARY FOR SUNDAYS AND FEASTS

✠

Harold Winstone

The Second Vatican Council decreed that "in sacred celebrations there is to be more reading from Holy Scripture, and it is to be more varied and suitable" and in particular in the Mass "the treasures of the Bible are to be opened more lavishly so that richer fare may be provided for the faithful at the table of God's word. In this way a more representative portion of the Holy Scriptures will be read to the people over a set cycle of years"[1]

In conformity with these regulations a whole new lectionary was devised. The previous Mass Lectionary provided an Epistle and Gospel for every Sunday of the year, which meant that on any particular Sunday each year the Scripture readings were the same. The faithful became familiar with these readings, and, with the passing of the years, possibly over-familiar, especially when they realised that on any particular Sunday the type of sermon that was preached became predictable.

So two far-reaching changes were introduced: a three-yearly cycle of readings, and the addition of an Old Testament reading which bore some kind of relationship to the Gospel reading.

Two principles govern the selection of readings. There is a thematic principle, used during Advent, Lent and Easter, when the particular spirit of the season is emphasised in all the readings; and a principle of semi-continuous reading used for the thirty-four Sundays of the Year which do not have a distinct liturgical spirit. On these days the readings from the letters and from the Gospel are more or less continuous, and the Old Testament reading is chosen to harmonise with the Gospel reading.

What follows is gleaned from the *Introduction to the New Roman Lectionary*, which is a model of lucidity.

Detailed analysis of the Lectionary

I *The season of Advent*

Each of the Sunday Gospel readings has a special note:
1st Sunday of Advent – the coming of the Lord at the end of time.
2nd and 3rd Sundays of Advent – John the Baptist.
4th Sunday of Advent – the events which immediately prepared for the birth of our Lord.
The Old Testament readings are prophecies about the Messiah and the Messianic times, especially those from Isaiah.

The readings from an apostle give exhortations and proclamations of faith suited to the spirit of the liturgical time of year.

II *Christmastide*

For the Vigil and the three Masses of Christmas the prophetic reading is taken from Isaiah. The texts are chosen from the Roman tradition which still persists in some local rites. Other readings, with two exceptions, are taken from the Roman Missal.

On the Sunday within the Octave of the Nativity, the Feast of the Holy Family, the Gospel treats of the infancy of Jesus and the other readings treat of family life.

On the Octave day of the Nativity and the Solemnity of Mary Mother of God, 1 January, the readings are about the Virgin Mother of God (Gospel and second reading) and about the giving of the holy name Jesus, a feast which is no longer in the Calendar (Gospel and first reading).

On the second Sunday after the Nativity the readings treat of the mystery of the Incarnation.

On the Epiphany the text from an apostle treats of the vocation of non-Christians to salvation.

On the Sunday after the Epiphany, the Feast of the Baptism of our Lord, the texts chosen are about this mystery.

III *Lent*

On the first and second Sundays of Lent the narratives of the temptation and of the transfiguration of Jesus are read from the synoptics.

On the third, fourth and fifth Sundays, Year 1, the Gospels of the Samaritan woman, the man born blind and Lazarus are read. These may also be read in Years 2 and 3 since they are important for Christian initiation. But for Year 2 there are also texts from John about the future glorification of Christ through the cross and resurrection; and for Year 3 there are texts from Luke about conversion.

The Old Testament readings are about the history of salvation, which is one of the subjects of the Lenten catechesis. In each year the series of texts gives the principal elements of that history from the beginning up to the promise of the new covenant; especially the readings about Abraham (second Sunday) and about the exodus (third Sunday).

The readings from an apostle are chosen so that they correspond to the Gospel and Old Testament readings, and, where possible, establish a closer connection between them.

IV *Paschal time*

The numbering of the Sundays after Easter has been revised. Low Sunday is now the second Sunday of Easter, and there are seven Sundays of Easter between Easter Sunday and Pentecost. Up to the third Sunday of Easter inclusive, the Gospel readings are about the appearances of the risen Christ. In order not to interrupt these, the readings about the Good Shepherd have been transferred to the fourth (formerly third) Sunday of Easter.

On the fifth, sixth, and seventh Sundays of Easter the Gospel readings are excerpts from the sermon and prayer of Christ at the Last Supper.

The first readings are taken from the Acts of the Apostles and are based on a three-year cycle following a parallel and progressive scheme. In this way something about the life, witness and growth of the early Church will be given each year.

The readings from an apostle are taken in Year 1 from the first letter of Peter; in Year 2 from the first letter of John; and in Year 3 from the Apocalypse. These texts seem most appropriate to the spirit of joyous faith and firm hope proper to the season.

V *The yearly cycle*

The Yearly Cycle is composed of thirty-three or thirty-four weeks which occur outside the seasons already dealt with. The Cycle begins on the Monday after the Sunday after 6 January, and goes on until the Tuesday before Ash Wednesday. It then begins again on the Monday after Pentecost Sunday and ends before first vespers of the first Sunday of Advent.

The Lectionary provides readings for the thirty-four Sundays and their subsequent weeks. However, sometimes there are only thirty-three weeks in the Yearly Cycle. Furthermore, each year some of the Sundays are proper to different seasons of the year e.g. the feast of the Baptism of our Lord and Pentecost Sunday; or are replaced regularly by a Solemnity e.g. the Holy Trinity, Christ the King.

To keep the order of the Yearly Cycle the following should be observed:

(a) The feast of the Baptism of our Lord on the Sunday after the Epiphany always takes the place of the first Sunday of the Year. Hence the Sunday after the feast of the Baptism of our Lord is the second Sunday of the Year. The other Sundays follow in sequence up to and including the Sunday before Ash Wednesday.

(b) After the seasons of Lent and Easter, the Yearly Cycle is resumed on the Monday after Pentecost Sunday in the following way:

If there are thirty-four Sundays in the Year, the week which immediately follows the week in which Lent began is the new starting point: e.g. if there were six weeks before Lent, on Pentecost Monday the readings for the Monday of the seventh week of the year are used, and the Yearly Cycle continues from then on. The Solemnity of the Holy Trinity will of course replace the Sunday at the beginning of the following week.

If there are thirty-three Sundays of the Year, the week which should have been the starting point on Pentecost Monday is omitted, and the Yearly Cycle is resumed with the week after that: e.g. if there were five weeks before Lent, on Pentecost Monday the readings for Monday of the seventh week of the year are used. Week six is omitted. This is to ensure that the eschatological texts are always read on the last two Sundays of the year.

The Gospel readings for the second Sunday of the Year treat of the ways in which our Lord revealed himself, the theme of the Epiphany. The traditional reading of the marriage feast of Cana is used for this, and also two other readings taken from the Gospel of John.

On the third Sunday of the Year, the semi-continuous reading of the three synoptic Gospels begins. This reading is so arranged as to give the teaching proper to each Gospel in the context of the development of the life and preaching of our Lord. (Year 1 is Matthew, Year 2 Mark, Year 3 Luke). In this way there is also a harmony established between the meaning of the Gospel and the development of the liturgical year. After the Epiphany, the narratives about our Lord's first preaching are read and these fit in well with the baptism and first manifestations of our Lord, which were the subjects of the readings on the Epiphany and subsequent Sundays. At the end of the liturgical year the eschatological themes come in their natural place.

In Year 2, after the sixteenth Sunday, readings from chapter six of John, the sermon on the bread of life, are inserted. This insertion comes naturally enough since the narrative of the multiplication of loaves in John takes the place of the same narrative in Mark. In Year 3 the semi-continuous reading of Luke is begun on the third Sunday with the Prologue of Luke, since this shows very aptly the author's intention and could not be read elsewhere.

The Old Testament readings are chosen in relation to the Gospel readings, in order to avoid too great a diversity of readings at each Mass and to show the unity of both testaments. Where possible the readings chosen are short and easy, but since they are chosen to fit the Gospel there is no sequence in them.

There is a semi-continuous reading of the letters of Paul and James, since the letters of Peter and John are read during Paschal time and at Christmas. Since the first letter to the Corinthians deals with many questions and is rather long, it is divided over the three-year cycle, at the beginning of each year. In the same way it seemed best to divide the letter to the Hebrews over two years, Years 2 and 3.

The readings for the thirty-fourth and last Sunday of the Year celebrate the Solemnity of Christ the King, foreshadowed by David, proclaimed amid the humiliations of the Passion and Cross, reigning in the Church, and to come again at the end of time.

NOTE

1 *Constitution on the Sacred Liturgy*, nos 35 and 51.

14

PREACHING IN THE LITURGY

Gordon S. Wakefield

Why Preach?

Preaching, that is proclamation, belongs to the very beginnings of Christianity and is so much part of its nature that,
without preaching, Christianity would be a different religion. "The medium is the message". There is a *skandalon*
here, for preaching may seem arrogant, incompatible with
the Servant-Messiah and the Servant-Church. "He shall
not strive, nor cry aloud, nor cause his voice to be heard in
the streets". And preaching demands hearers, prepared to
listen, to weigh and consider, but in the end to submit, perhaps on the impulse, without argument. It is often maintained that people in our time demand discussion, that they
wish to answer back and to participate orally in the quest
for truth. They prefer the dialectic of Socrates to the oracles
of Isaiah. Or, contrariwise, they find salvation in silence
without words, by contemplative techniques and the light
within.

There have been preachers who have hectored, bullied
and cowed their hearers into submission. They have over-
simplified issues and concealed the whole counsel of God.
They have misinterpreted Scripture, falsified history,
fudged morality, made their own indignation surrogate for
the wrath of God, denounced too screamingly, comforted
too soothingly, given offence too willingly, avoided offence
too sycophantically. They have vulgarised mystery, yet
obscured the "open secret" of God's grace. They have left
people in their sins, or made a motorway to hell for their

hearers and themselves. The casualties of preaching cannot be computed.

Yet Jesus himself came preaching, and so did all the apostles. No revival in the Church has been accomplished without preaching. The Protestant Reformation was a reformation of preaching; Wesley preached and founded an order of preachers; "the Oxford movement could be viewed as the rise of a company of mission preachers"; the liturgical movement has rediscovered the primitive unity of Word and Sacrament. No longer may Catholic priests be held up to Protestant horror and scorn as "non-preachers".

The reason is obvious. Christianity is first and foremost not a philosophy of life but the announcement of good news. And it is good news of God, to whom human reason may point, but who is ultimately neither proved nor disproved by metaphysics, but by the breaking in of his love and goodness to a world in which they are often denied by the evil and futility woven into the very scheme of things.

As is so fashionable to assert these days, the gospel is a story to be told. The preacher is like Browning's St. John in *A Death in the Desert*:

To me, that story – ay that Life and Death
Of which I wrote "it was" – to me, it is;
– Is, here and now; I apprehend nought else.
Is not God now i' the world His Power first made?
Is not His love at issue with sin
Visibly when a wrong is done on earth?
Love, wrong and pain, what see I else around?
Yea and the Resurrection and Uprise
To the right hand of the throne – what is it beside,
When such truth, breaking bounds, o'erfloods my soul,
And, as I saw the sin and death, even so
See I the need yet transiency of both,
The good and glory consummated thence?

The story is not made-up by the teller. It is glad tidings of great joy, passed on from age-to-age, told with imagination, compassion, and knowledge of our humanity, but in origin something given and to be received. The Word, like the Sacrament, is a miracle of grace, not perpetually to be analysed or argued with; it is beyond our invention or contriving, and equally we say "Take . . .". "He who has ears to hear, let him hear".

Preaching implies conviction. This must not be, as sometimes, a forced and bogus conviction, "argument weak, shout like hell". The preacher must not appear infallible, removed for the nonce from the sphere of human infirmity, immune to doubt and free from sin. He will be aware of difficulties. C. J. Cadoux once claimed that the Pauline equivalent of "Thus saith the Lord" is "I am persuaded", and Dennis Nineham has said that the homiletic conclusion for him is often "This is how I see it. What about you?" The preacher at times may appear to struggle, to be wrestling with his theme. It is surprising how often hesitations, broken sentences and a sense of incommunicable mystery may betoken the most effective sermons. Something too easy, fluent, dogmatic may be inadequate both to the gospel and to human life. But the preacher must speak from the heart and mind in unison, and though his faith be as a grain of mustard seed it must be pitted against the mountains of sin, error and indifference. He will have to state the paradoxes of grace most of all when he speaks from the depths of his own sin, and offers to others a forgiveness which only with fear and trembling may he claim for himself. Like Bunyan, he will speak what he feels, what he smartingly does feel, and yet what rests on far more than his own emotions.

> The Voice that rolls the stars along,
> Speaks all the promises.

There is that in Christianity which can be conveyed by the Word alone, in majesty, uninterrupted, which is debased by a chat-show and loses splendour through audio-visual aids.

The Word proclaimed by a solitary voice may have an austerity and a purity which conveys the "infinite qualitative difference" as well as the intimacy of God; which, although there is beauty of sound, does not beguile or live by sensual delights, yet arouses consciousness of the mystery of the God who is better addressed than expressed, and who is beyond the time or space which the visual arts demand. W. H. Auden once commented on Goethe's assertion:

> We ought to talk less and draw more. I, personally, should like to renounce speech altogether and, like organic nature, communicate everything I have to say in sketches.

Goethe, said Auden, knew that this was an exaggeration. "A drawing can show what something is at a moment, but it cannot show how it came to be that way or what will happen to it next; this only language can do".

But when this is recognised, it has to be admitted that the conditions of modern life do not make preaching as natural or as easy as it has been for much of Church history. The media bombard us with words and we do not listen, letting the radio blare with profound wisdom or utter inanity, with hilarious humour or sob-stories, while we go on with our own chatter. It is hard to preach in the open air, to attract crowds for proclamation unless the preacher is something of a crank, or a Sunday afternoon sensation, or a charismatic Pope, on whose words the faithful and the sympathetic hang. Billy Graham has filled stadiums and won response, though the impact of his rallies on society at large, rather than those seeking to be converted in this way, is not evident.

Liturgical preaching

The liturgy gives at once the best hearing for the preacher today, and goes back to the roots of the proclamation in the life of the people of God. Scripture and tradition illustrate this. The walk to Emmaus is a union of word and sacrament; the disciples' hearts were warmed for the revelation of the risen Christ by his exposition of the Scriptures. Paul preached long at Troas; the young man Eutyches fell asleep and out of the window, Paul revived him, seemingly dead, and then continued with the Eucharist. Justin Martyr (c. 150) in his account of the Eucharist to the Roman Emperor says that a discourse "exhorting and astonishing us to imitate these good things" follows the reading of the records of the apostles and the writings of the apostles. The *Book of Common Prayer* prescribes a sermon only at the Holy Communion. In the Roman Catholic Church since Vatican II, preaching at the Sunday Mass is obligatory.

This type of preaching demands skills all its own. There are seeming difficulties and disadvantages. The Sermon, placed early in the liturgical action, may become obliterated by what follows. There is much more chance of comment from the departing congregation if it concludes the service. It may lose something of its power if it is not climactic. There will be intercessions to take us into the world, and possibly notices before we join in the solemnities of the Sacrament. There may even be conflict between sermon and prayers if these are not from the same voice. And time is limited, so that the preacher may resort to a few unprepared platitudes, or read a short paragraph or two, or make the people dizzy with too many ideas, insufficiently expounded.

Yet each of these necessities and constraints may be turned to glorious gain. All that follows the sermon should be seen as response to it. Jesus led his disciples down from the Mount of Transfiguration to the sordid scene beneath, and so, through the trivialities and the tragedies of Church and world, to the way of the Cross and the glory beyond. And this should be the progress of the liturgy.

There are certain rules for preaching at the liturgy:

(1) The preacher must cultivate economy of time and words and style. There are signs that we are breaking free of the shackles of a mere sixty minutes for worship. The preacher ought to be able to reckon on fifteen minutes. This means that there cannot be the luxury of anecdotal illustration, which for the old Central Hall preachers were not only oratorical tours de force and an educational method, but could make three quarters of an hour seem as a few minutes to their hearers. Yet illustration there must be to bring life and colour to what may otherwise be expository or doctrinal abstraction. The advantages of brevity must be exploited. There must be some sense of urgency, though not of hectic haste; but each Eucharist is a unique opportunity, never to be repeated; the preacher does speak "as a dying man to dying men"; or, to use a different metaphor from

previous generations, there is "ten minutes to wake the dead". Clarity and incisiveness are essential, and a short space may make possible a power and intensity which could not be sustained for too long. Some of the greatest sermons of the years since the last war have been fairly short, notably Paul Tillich and Austin Farrer.

(2) The preacher must neither be over-excited nor too restrained. It may be that he will speak most to his hearers' condition when he is not too self-consciously stirred. Tears may have been shed in the study; they may not be infrequent in preparation because of the ineffable wonder of Divine grace; they will rarely be apparent in the pulpit. Yet a sermon should inspire its hearers with a sense of the numinous; it should be like the "perspective-glass", which Bunyan's pilgrims held with trembling hands at the Delectable Mountains, and saw "something like a gate and also some of the glory of the place". The Liturgy will save the sermon from sentimental indulgence, for the Service will proceed and reach its climax in the bread which is Christ's body and the wine which is his blood, and which inebriates more soberly than rhetoric, and where emotion is governed by austerity.

(3) The sermon will, as a rule, be expository, in that it will follow from the Scriptures which have just been heard. The Joint Liturgical Group lectionary for the Eucharist indicates controlling passages for different seasons of the year – Old Testament leading up to Christmas, Gospel until Pentecost, and then Epistle; it also provides themes for the Sundays. These last are of somewhat dubious value, for they may make a preacher deal with them rather than the Scriptures themselves, and to look for the themes in the lessons, rather than by wrestling with the Scriptures to win their message for himself and the people. He should not feel tied too slavishly to the controlling passages, though part of their virtue is that they will bring to his notice parts of the Bible, which he might, even on the days when they are set, be tempted to avoid. Sometimes he will be able to link all three readings in the sermon, and this is on occasion a good way of liturgical preaching. But it must not be felt to be obligatory, nor be forced. Faithful and honest exegesis is

called for and its discipline is demanding. The Bible is not always "plain truth for plain people". And it may contain different levels of meaning. To ask what it meant to those who first wrote, read or heard it, is not always the best way to find the truth as it is in Jesus for men and women of the twentieth-century. It is often instructive to learn from those of "the third world" who read Scripture out of poverty and oppression and are innocent of historical criticism. Nor can we ignore the tradition, the way in which the Bible has spoken to our ancestors in the faith. Some today plead for a return to allegory and typology as in the Eastern tradition or in the sermons of Bishop Kenneth Kirk, *The Fourth River*, for instance. It may help to remember that much of the New Testament and of the Old began as preaching and that Christ comes to us not only as a preacher himself, who would never have been crucified had he kept silent, but as one who preached from the beginning.

(4) Preaching is not only proclamation. It not only is the fruit of the preacher's own meditation, but it may correspond in structure to this classic form of prayer, as in the *Spiritual Exercises* of St. Ignatius – an introductory "composition of place" as the gospel scene or prophetic epistolary background is vividly described; the drawing out of certain points of application to our lives; and a concluding resolve, the aim always in some sense conversion. There should always be a pause when the preacher has finished. There may sometimes be "a silence which can be felt". (Slovenly endings are much to be deplored). The meditation may lead to a contemplative consummation in the Eucharist in which we are led from distant vision to the eternal reality itself.

The preacher may seem to be guilty of a lack of honesty and realism. He offers a life to which he aspires but does not attain and which, he knows, cannot be lived in this world as it is. The more visionary the preacher, the less realistic he will appear. Hearers may be much edified, or inspired, they may feel a shiver down the spine as when at a solemn music – and preaching should be lyrical with something of the ground bass in it, as well as hortatory and in a measure didactic; but they go out to business as usual, to a world of aggressive competition, political accommodation, and involvement in the commerce and industry of death. Short of being revolutionaries, which is everywhere fraught with terrible risks of the last error being worse than the first, they have no alternative. If they heeded the preaching as seriously as they ought, the tension would be unbearable.

One of the great qualities of the Anglican Biblical theologian, Sir Edwyn Hoskyns, was that he never forgot who his hearers were, and, therefore, like Scripture itself, and rather more than this chapter might seem to advocate, he eschewed mystical flights. He preached the Word. His sermons, in Corpus Christi College Chapel in Cambridge, which belong to the years between the wars, are perhaps too fearful of millenial hopes and political reform, too sceptical of peace movements and creative evolution. The nuclear age might vindicate his theology, or call for greater faith in what humanity must boldly do to seek to save itself. Yet he spoke with evangelical realism to an audience, predominantly male, in words which conclude a series published years after his death under the title, *We are the Pharisees*:

You are not to dream through life; you are not to wander about with no roots anywhere; you are not cosmopolitan gentlemen floating about; you are grounded in the earth, men of the world. That is, however, but one side of the truth. We can be overwhelmed by the world, crushed by it, in bondage under its elements. But we are Christians engaged in a struggle between the flesh and the spirit, called to be sons of God by Christ, in the world, yet not of it. We do not worship a disembodied spirit. We worship the Christ. We eat his body and drink his blood (crude though the language may seem, the truth of the Christian religion is there). Flesh and blood controlled by the Spirit of God and brought into submission to the will of God is the life of the Church. And this is your salvation and mine, a salvation grounded upon a tension which is never resolved in this life.

But Christian hope, based upon belief in God and upon the return of Jesus to the Father, declares that the tension will be resolved, not by death but in life eternal.

"In my Father's house are many mansions; if it were not so, I would have told you". But more important words for us here and now run thus: "I pray not that thou shouldest take them out of the world, but that thou shouldest keep them from the evil ... Sanctify them through thy truth".

15

RESPONSE TO THE WORD

✠

J. C. Stewart

To be addressed is to be accounted responsible – liable (and, therefore, able) to make a response. Human responsibility arises in the first place from man's being addressed by God. God's address is to be heard and acted upon (James 1.22). His word is not to return to him empty but is to accomplish that which he purposes (Isaiah 55.11). Yet that does not happen in a mechanical and inevitable way. Failure to respond is recognised as a possibility (Romans 10.16). The fitting response is the response of faith and freely-given obedience. This address/response pattern is the pattern of the whole Christian life. It is reflected in several of the New Testament letters where the declaration of God's revelation and communication of himself to humanity is followed by an exhortation to, and indication of, appropriate response. In the case of the Letter to the Romans this response is described as "your spiritual worship" (12.1, RSV), though it clearly encompasses the whole of life.

Worship more narrowly defined, the Divine Service, is the liturgical intensification and anticipation of that life pattern, therefore it is characteristic of the *first* day of the week. Our concern here is with the response element in that liturgy. Because it is response, it cannot stand on its own. It is totally dependent on the antecedent Word of God and without strict attention to that Word it would simply be an exercise in human arrogance. The nature of that Word and the means by which it is communicated are, therefore, matters to which attention must be paid. The Bible itself is frequently (not least in liturgical formulations) referred to as "the Word of God" and Martin Luther, for one, declared that "the preaching of the Word of God is the Word of God". Should we, then, expect to read off the appropriate response in a simple and direct way from scripture and sermon? There has been a tradition within Protestantism, based on a literalist view of scripture as having, directly, the authority of God, which has maintained that only what is commanded in the Bible is permitted in worship. It has resulted in much unnecessary barrenness in worship and we do not believe that it is a tenable view. But neither would we wish to be committed to the opposite view that anything is permitted which is not specifically forbidden. The citing of scripture above is an indication that we believe it to have a positive, and not merely a negative, authority. That authority is based on the inseparable relationship of scripture to the Word of God, but does not imply that the living Word of God has been fossilised in the words of scripture. What are required are "ears to hear" and a willingness to be obedient. What is provided is not a rule of thumb.

Liturgical response is also totally dependent on the presence and work of the Spirit as the means by which scripture and preaching are discerned to 'convey' the Word of God, and also as that which gives form to the response, for "we do not even know how we ought to pray, but through our inarticulate groans the Spirit himself is pleading for us" (Romans 8.26). The element of *epiclesis* is essential. At the heart of the response lies the prayer "Your kingdom come", for the responding church recognises that the time of totally loving and obedient response is not yet, and even (or, especially) in Divine Service we are unprofitable servants.

And, finally, the liturgical response to the Word recognises its own incompleteness. At its conclusion it says, "Go forth ..." lest the vital connection of liturgy and life be lost.

How is this liturgical response to be articulated? How is it to relate to the scriptural and preached word which has preceded it? What elements are to find a place in it? It is a response of faith, of gratitude, of loving obedience. It is

132

expressed in affirmations of faith; in songs and prayers of praise and gifts of gratitude; and in prayers of concern and commitment. (Dietrich Bonhoeffer's biographer notes that he took so seriously the claim that the preached word was to be received in humility as the Word of God that he would not permit the response of critical analysis even to the sermons of his students when they were preached before a congregation).

Most of the main stream of Christian tradition agrees that "the Liturgy of the Upper Room" provides the fullest and most appropriate response to the Word. It is here, responding to the Word which called it into being and constantly reforms it, and invoking the Spirit from which it derives its life, that the church is seen most truly as church. As it gathers at the Table it finds a setting in which the various elements of its response may most adequately be held together. Yet it has also to be recognised that there are situations in which weekly communion is unlikely to be achieved in the immediate future, for, despite the fact that such an achievement would be the realisation of a Reformation aim, there is a strong feeling that it is "un-Protestant". The best that may be hoped for in some places, at least in the short term, is that non-sacramental services at the main weekly gathering of the congregation should have a basically eucharistic pattern. Where that is the case most of what follows will be of fairly obvious applicability.

Affirmations of faith

The classic affirmations of faith are the Catholic Creeds. Whether or not they were originally intended for liturgical use, it would be difficult to argue against the fittingness of responding, at least on occasion, to the proclamation of the Word by rising to declare "I believe" or "We believe" or, alternatively, of making such a declaration of shared faith the immediate preliminary to the actions at the Table. The form in which the Creeds give expression to faith is not without its significance for their liturgical use. They are, in their major emphasis, cast in the form of affirmations of trust in the persons of the Godhead rather than of assent to doctrines concerning these persons. Those who use them are pledging the commitment of will and affections rather than outlining a systematic theology.

It has been contended that, where the mighty acts of God are to be fully rehearsed in the course of the Great Prayer, it is otiose to have them in their credal form. If the argument is felt to have substance, hymnody may provide an alternative means of direct affirmation, as may such brief acclamations as are to be found in *The Daily Office – Revised*. The scope of such affirmations may be less wide than that of the Creeds but they may be more particularly related to the thrust of one or more of the lections of the day. For example, the *Worship Book* (UPCUSA) provides a form, largely scriptural, suitable especially for the Easter season. Likewise, if denominational traditions allow such freedom, the lections may directly provide the basis for the construction of brief *ad hoc* affirmations. For example, on Pentecost 2, year 1 (*JLG Lectionary*) 1 Peter 2.9, 10 might be repeated in the first person or, on Pentecost 9, year 2, the father's declaration in Mark 9.24 might be reiterated. Very often, however, contemporary affirmations of faith take the form of assertions of doctrine. It remains important to provide for the articulation of commitment.

Intercessions

If faith without works is dead, affirmations of faith unrelated to prayers of concern must be considered suspect. To respond to God is, inescapably, to respond to our brother (1 John 4.20, 21) and to the whole world of God's creation. It may not always be easy to strike a balance between our brother (a high degree of particularity which causes grievance or disappointment by what it seems to exclude) and the whole world (wide generalities which fail to stimulate, or give expression to, deep concern on the part of the worshippers). Since we are here concerned not merely with response to the Word in general but with response to the Word in the particular form in which it comes to us on any given Sunday, as determined by the lectionary system in use, it may be suggested that the direction of at least some of the intercessions should be guided by what has been heard from the scriptures and the sermon. Such *JLG Lectionary* themes as, e.g., "Christ the Teacher" and "Christ the Healer" (9 and 8 before Easter) rather obviously suggest that the intercessions on these days should concentrate in greater than usual detail on the teaching profession and the healing professions and on the institutions in which they operate; but these themes may also give a particular direction to intercessions for the church, for homes and parents, and for the state, in their concern for education and health.

Offerings

"The necessity for generous giving was recognised by the first Christians as the right response to Christ's own self-giving (2 Corinthians 8.9). The presentation of these gifts early became an integral part of worship" (*Dictionary of Liturgy and Worship, sub.* "Alms"). Such offerings relate naturally to intercession and provide a means of "putting our money where our mouth is". Any suggestions that "filthy lucre" should not find a place near the heart of Christian worship is to be resisted as betraying a tendency either to disjoin the liturgical response to the Word from the larger response in daily life or to confine that response to realms supposedly more spiritual. In liturgical practice such alms may well be linked with the oblations necessary to make provision for the Lord's table. Only irregularly, however, will there be any direct link with the lections for the day, and while the reciting of an appropriate scriptural text in connection with the collection of the offerings might serve to heighten the responsive nature of alms giving, the too frequent quotation of isolated texts of scripture throughout the service can create a false impression of the nature of the Word and the authority of scripture.

Eucharist and Eucharistic Prayers

Although the *Faith and Order* document on *Baptism, Eucharist and Ministry* uses the term Eucharist to encompass preparation, proclamation and response as a whole, the word is used here to refer simply to those parts which fall within the "four-action shape" of Dom Gregory Dix. ("He took, he gave thanks, he broke, he gave"). The Eucharist, thus narrowly defined, has a two-fold relation to the Word.

1. It is response.
    (a) It is response to what is recorded as the dominical word at the Last Supper: "This do". The Reformed practice of immediately prefacing the four-fold action with the narrative of institution make this particularly clear but all liturgies relate unmistakably, by more or less verbatim quotation, to one or other of the biblical accounts of the Last Supper.
    (b) It is, however, more than a response of imitative action to a particular word. As sacrament it depends on and responds to the whole range of the creative and incarnate Word.
    (c) In the eucharistic prayer itself the practice of providing proper prefaces means that, at least at those seasons and feasts for which such provision is made, there will be emphasis on a theme drawn from or related to the particular "word" of the day. The range of such proper prefaces, so that thanksgiving is always related, without being confined, to the day's "word", might well be extended by their provision either by authority or *ex tempore*.

2. It is communicative and confirmative of the Word. "It is certainly true that we get . . . no other thing in the sacrament than we get in the Word. For what more would you ask than truly to receive the Son of God himself? . . . Why then is the sacrament appointed? Not that you may get any new thing but that you may get the same thing better than you had it in the Word . . . a better hold of Christ . . . The Sacraments also serve to seal up and confirm the truth that is in the Word". The provision in the *Alternative Service Book* of post-communion sentences, either drawn from the earlier lections or reiterating their dominant theme, may be taken as a strengthening of this aspect of the sacrament, though it

may be open to the danger noted above in the use of isolated texts.

The Lord's Prayer

The Lord's Prayer is appropriately used as a kind of summation of the Great Prayer. Its themes – God, his kingdom, bread, forgiveness, – are central themes of the Gospel which gives rise to our worship.

Peace

The Letter to the Ephesians characterises the word proclaimed by Jesus as "peace to you who were far off and peace to those who were near by". And, according to the Fourth Gospel, that peace was his "parting gift" at the Last Supper and the particular greeting of his resurrection appearances. The deliberate sharing of the peace of Christ within the Christian fellowship gathered at the Table is, then, an appropriate response to a central element in his ministry.

Dismissal and blessing

Even those parts of the church which favour prescription in liturgical matters now make allowance for considerable variation here, mainly on a seasonal basis. The congregation may be sent out, and blessing sought, on the grounds of some aspect of the divine character or action of which the readings for the day have spoken. There seems little reason why the principle should not be extended to all Sundays where it may be done without undue contrivance. And especially if there has been no earlier sharing of peace, it may very properly find a place in the dismissal or benediction.

Other forms of response

Despite Karl Barth's suggestion that a complete act of worship would begin with Baptism and conclude with Communion, it may be thought better that Baptism and services of benediction, such as Confirmation, should be treated as other forms of response to the Word. Peter understands the new birth, of which Baptism is the sacrament, as being thus related to the Word. (It has been suggested that 1 Peter is a baptismal homily). He says: "You have been born anew, not of mortal parentage but of immortal, through the living and enduring word of God ... this "word" is the word of the Gospel preached to you". (1.23, 25).

To conclude

This chapter has been written to reflect the broad pattern of a diet of worship as preparation, proclamation, and response, but that is a pattern which is repeated on a smaller scale several times in the course of the service. It may well begin with a call to worship to which the preparatory rite of invocation and confession is responsive. The main readings may well have a responsive punctuation of psalmody. Other instances have been noted above.

On a broader scale the whole of the church's worship, including the element of proclamation, may be regarded as response to the prevenient Word of God in Christ. Indeed, it is important so to regard it, and not as a matter of merely human initiative and contrivance.

16

THE LITURGY AFTER THE LITURGY

✠

Victor L. Hunter

The liturgy ends, "Go in peace to love and serve the Lord".
As the liturgy of corporate worship ends so another liturgy
begins. It is the liturgy after the liturgy. Or, more accurately, it is the continuation of the liturgy of the church
gathered (*ecclesia*) in the life of the church scattered in the
world (*diaspora*). For both the corporate worship of the
church, and the life of the church lived in the world are
liturgy – a word that originally meant a public work undertaken by a person at private cost. It came to be used, in
both the Greek Old Testament and New Testament, of
religious services or rituals performed, but was again
broadened in the New Testament, to be used of the way life
is lived in active faith and obedient service to God in the
world (cf. Acts 13.2; Romans 15.16, 27; 2 Corinthians 9.12;
Philippians 2.17, 25; Hebrews 8.6; 9.21).

In popular understanding today, the term liturgy is often
thought to refer solely to the order and/or the text of the
prayers, confessions, creeds and eucharist of the public
worship of the church. In the same way, the term worship is
often thought to refer to acts of devotion or religious piety
offered either privately or in the public Services of the
church. In the New Testament there is, however, a cluster
of seven or eight words for the concept of worship that
range in meaning from reverence, awe and devotion, to service, life style, giving and social action. By recapturing the
broader New Testament understanding of worship, liturgy
and life will be seen not as two separate realities (one sacred

139

and the other secular) but as two dimensions of a single reality.

Worship is the "way of being in the world" for the Christian community. *Worship is everything the Christian congregation does.* This affirmation is not intended to place a limitation on Christian involvement in the world. Rather, it is to expand its understanding of liturgy to include the whole arena of Christian living. Any renewal of liturgy is at heart, therefore, a renewal of the life of the church in the world.

While it is crucial to connect worship to life, it is equally important that the life of the church in the world be rooted in corporate worship. The liturgy of corporate worship is the church's native soil. No amount of Christian social action can replace corporate worship any more than corporate worship can substitute for the "love of the neighbour" in the daily life of the Christian. Christian identity, cohesive community, and spiritual sensitivity will wither and die without corporate worship. The Church centres its life in the celebration of the "first day" for the sake of its solidarity in the "six days". The corporate liturgy of prayer, praise, preaching, confession and communion on the Lord's day prepares it for the liturgy of service, witness and priesthood in the Lord's week. The kiss of peace, passed to brother and sister in the liturgy of the Sunday worship, moves on to become the embrace of love to the broader society in the liturgy of daily life. The body of Christ (the church) in the world is ultimately nourished by the body of Christ given and shared in the sacrament of corporate worship.

Christian worship and Christian living constitute a single liturgy. They are a seamless garment of Christ's presence in the world. There are aspects of this liturgy which belong to corporate worship. Christ is present in Word and Sacrament. The story of his presence is learned, the word of his presence is heard, the life of his presence is received. Then there are aspects of this liturgy which belong to life lived in the world. These are the acts of faith and obedience to the Way, and the ways of Christ, among men and women. Corporate worship will send Christians into the world to love and serve; life in the world will send Christians back to corporate worship in need, in thanksgiving, and in praise. So the body of Christ that is broken into the world on the "six days" is raised again in wholeness on the "first day". The one liturgy – Christ's presence in the world (Hebrews 8.6) – is celebrated "in all times and in all places" by those who are "in Him".